Essential French

Edited by

Shaina Malkin and Christine Boucher

Published in the United States by Living Language, an imprint of Random House, Inc.

www.livinglanguage.com

Editor: Shaina Malkin
Production Editor: Carolyn Roth
Production Manager: Tom Marshall
Interior Design: Sophie Chin
Illustrations: Sophie Chin

First Edition

ISBN: 978-0-307-97153-1

This book is available at special discounts for bulk purchases for sales promotions or premiums. Special editions, including personalized covers, excerpts of existing books, and corporate imprints, can be created in large quantities for special needs. For more information, write to Special Markets/ Premium Sales, 1745 Broadway, MD 3-1, New York, New York 10019 or e-mail specialmarkets@ randomhouse.com.

PRINTED IN THE UNITED STATES OF AMERICA

10 9 8

Acknowledgments

Thanks to the Living Language team: Amanda D'Acierno, Christopher Warnasch, Suzanne McQuade, Laura Riggio, Erin Quirk, Shaina Malkin, Amanda Munoz, Fabrizio La Rocca, Siobhan O'Hare, Sophie Chin, Sue Daulton, Alison Skrabek, Carolyn Roth, Ciara Robinson, Linda Schmidt, and Tom Marshall.

How to Use This Course 6

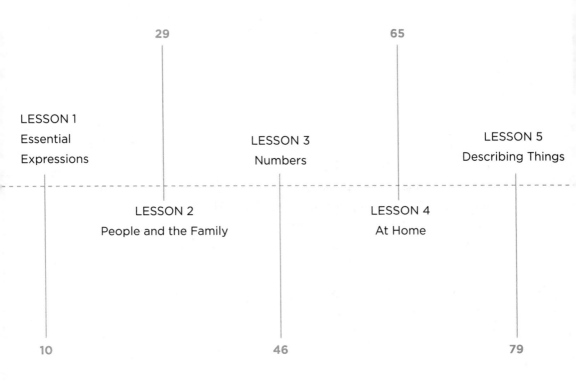

COURSE

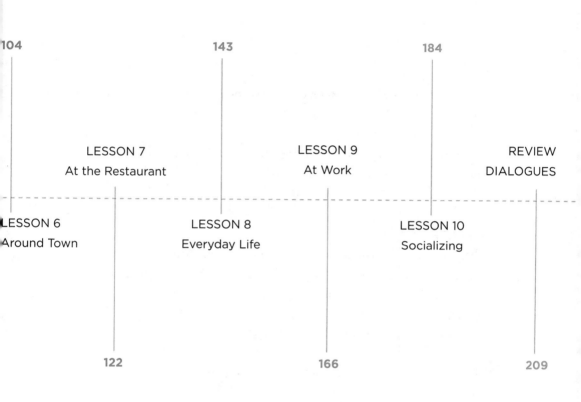
OUTLINE

How to Use This Course

Bonjour !

Welcome to *Living Language Essential French*! Ready to learn how to speak, read, and write French?

Before we begin, let's go over what you'll see in this course. It's very easy to use, but this section will help you get started.

PHONETICS

The first five lessons of this course contain phonetics (in other words, [bah-geht] in addition to **baguette**) to help you get started with French pronunciation. However, please keep in mind that phonetics are not exact—they are just a general approximation of sounds—and thus you should rely most on the audio, *not* the phonetics, to further your pronunciation skills.

For a guide to our phonetics system, see the Pronunciation Guide at the end of the course.

LESSONS

There are 10 lessons in this course. Each lesson is divided into three parts and has the following components:

- **Welcome** at the beginning outlining what you will cover in each of the three parts of the lesson.

PART 1

- **Vocabulary Builder 1** listing the key words and phrases for that lesson.

- **Vocabulary Practice 1** to practice what you learned in Vocabulary Builder 1.

- **Grammar Builder 1** to guide you through the structure of the French language (how to form sentences, questions, and so on).

PART 2

- **Vocabulary Builder 2** listing more key words and phrases.

- **Vocabulary Practice 2** to practice what you learned in Vocabulary Builder 2.

- **Grammar Builder 2** for more information on language structure.

- **Work Out 1** for a comprehensive practice of what you've learned so far.

PART 3

- **Bring It All Together** to put what you've learned in a conversational context through a dialogue, monologue, description, or other similar text.

- **Work Out 2** for another helpful practice exercise.

- **Drive It Home** to ingrain an important point of French structure for the long term.

- **Parting Words** outlining what you learned in the lesson.

TAKE IT FURTHER

- **Take It Further** sections scattered throughout the lesson to provide extra information about the new vocabulary you just saw, expand on some grammar points, or introduce additional words and phrases.

WORD RECALL

- **Word Recall** sections appear in between lessons. They review important vocabulary and grammar from previous lessons, including the one you just finished. These sections will reinforce what you've learned so far in the course, and help you retain the information for the long term.

QUIZZES

This course contains two quizzes: **Quiz 1** is halfway through the course (after Lesson 5), and **Quiz 2** appears after the last lesson (Lesson 10). The quizzes are self-graded so it's easy for you to test your progress and see if you should go back and review.

REVIEW DIALOGUES

There are five **Review Dialogues** at the end of the course, after Quiz 2. These everyday dialogues review what you learned in Lessons 1-10, introduce some new vocabulary and structures, and allow you to become more familiar with conversational French. Each dialogue is followed by comprehension questions that serve as the course's final review.

PROGRESS BAR

You will see a **Progress Bar** on almost every page that has course material. It indicates your current position in the course and lets you know how much progress you're making. Each line in the bar represents a lesson, with the final line representing the Review Dialogues.

AUDIO

Look for this symbol ⏵ to help guide you through the audio as you're reading the book. It will tell you which track to listen to for each section that has audio. When you see the symbol, select the indicated track and start listening! If you don't see the symbol, then there isn't any audio for that section. You'll also see ⏸, which will tell you where that track ends.

The audio can be used on its own—in other words, without the book—when you're on the go. Whether in your car or at the gym, you can listen to the audio to brush up on your pronunciation, review what you've learned in the book, or even use it as a standalone course.

PRONUNCIATION GUIDE, GRAMMAR SUMMARY, GLOSSARY

At the back of this book you will find a **Pronunciation Guide**, **Grammar Summary**, and **Glossary**. The Pronunciation Guide provides information on French pronunciation and the phonetics system used in this course. The Grammar Summary contains a helpful, brief overview of key points in the French grammar system. It is also includes a **Grammar Index**, which lists the principal grammar topics covered in this course and where to find them in the book. The Glossary (French-English and English-French) includes all of the essential words from the ten lessons, as well as additional key vocabulary.

FREE ONLINE TOOLS

Go to *www.livinglanguage.com/languagelab* to access your free online tools. The tools are organized around the lessons in this course, with audiovisual flashcards, and interactive games and quizzes. These tools will help you to review and practice the vocabulary and grammar that you've seen in the lessons, as well provide some extra words and phrases related to the lesson's topic.

Lesson 1: Essential Expressions

Leçon un : les expressions essentielles

luh-soh(n) uh(n): lay zehks-preh-syoh(n) eh-sah(n)-syehl

Bienvenue ! [bya(n)-vuh-new] *Welcome!* In this first lesson, you'll learn basic courtesy expressions and other useful words and phrases that will get you started speaking French. You will learn how to:

1 Greet someone and ask how they're doing
Address someone formally and informally

2 Introduce yourself
Respond when people ask *How are you?*

3 Use what you've learned when
meeting people for the first time

Remember to look for this symbol ⓞ to help guide you through the audio as you're reading the book. It will tell you which track to listen to for each section that has audio. When you see the symbol, select the indicated track and start listening! If you don't see the symbol, then there isn't any audio for that section. You'll also see ⓘ, which will tell you where that track ends. Finally, keep in mind that the audio can also be used on its own when you're on the go!

So, let's begin with some essential vocabulary. Ready?

1 Greet someone and ask how they're doing
Address someone formally and informally

Vocabulary Builder 1

You'll see phonetics in the first five lessons of *Essential French* to help you get started. For a guide to the phonetics system used here, see the Pronunciation Guide at the end of the course.

▶ 1B Vocabulary Builder 1 (CD 1, Track 2)

Hello.	**Bonjour.**	boh(n)-zhoor
Hi. (can also mean Bye.)	**Salut.**	sah-lew
Good-bye.	**Au revoir.**	oh ruh-vwahr
How are you? (familiar)	**Comment vas-tu ?***	koh-mah(n) vah-tew
How are you? (polite)	**Comment allez-vous ?**	koh-mah(n) tah-lay-voo
I'm fine.	**Ça va.**	sah vah
What's your name? (familiar)	**Comment t'appelles-tu ?**	koh-mah(n) tah-pehl-tew
What's your name? (polite)	**Comment vous appelez-vous ?**	koh-mah(n) voo zah-play-voo
ma'am, madam, Mrs., Ms.	**madame**	mah-dahm
sir, Mr.	**monsieur**	muh-syuh
miss	**mademoiselle**	mahd-mwah-zehl

* In writing, French usually adds a space before the punctuation marks ! ? : and ;. As a result, you will see **Comment vas-tu ?** and not **Comment vas-tu?**

✎ Vocabulary Practice 1

Now let's practice what you've learned!

Fill in the blanks with the correct French translations of the following English phrases. Always feel free to use a dictionary or the glossary if you need to.

Hello. _____

Hi./Bye. _____

Good-bye. _____

How are you? (familiar) _____

How are you? (polite) _____

I'm fine. _____

What's your name? (familiar) _____

What's your name? (polite) _____

ma'am, madam, Mrs., Ms. _____

sir, Mr. _____

miss _____

ANSWER KEY:
Bonjour. (*Hello.*); Salut. (*Hi./Bye.*); Au revoir. (*Good-bye.*); Comment vas-tu ? (*How are you?,* [*familiar*]); Comment allez-vous ? (*How are you?, polite*); Ça va. (*I'm fine.*); Comment t'appelles-tu ? (*What's your name?, familiar*); Comment vous appelez-vous ? (*What's your name?,* [*polite*]); madame (*ma'am, madam, Mrs., Ms.*); monsieur (*sir, Mr.*); mademoiselle (*miss*)

Grammar Builder 1

▶ 1C Grammar Builder 1 (CD 1, Track 3)

Okay, let's stop there. (Listen to the audio for a quick, audio-only review of the terms you just learned!)

Did you notice that there are two ways of asking how someone is or what someone's name is?

One is familiar (informal), used with friends, family, and children. Those are the questions with the word tu [tew], which is the familiar way of saying *you*:

Comment vas-tu ?
How are you?

Comment t'appelles-tu ?
What's your name?

The others use the polite (formal) form for *you*: vous [voo]. It is used with adults you don't know well, colleagues (particularly supervisors), and people in formal situations:

Comment allez-vous ?
How are you?

Comment vous appelez-vous ?
What's your name?

So, in French, tu and vous both mean *you*, but the first is familiar and the second is polite. When in doubt, use vous unless you're invited to use tu.

To summarize:

FAMILIAR (INFORMAL)	POLITE (FORMAL)
tu (you)	vous (you)
Comment vas-tu ? (How are you?)	Comment allez-vous ? (How are you?)
Comment t'appelles-tu ? (What's your name?)	Comment vous appelez-vous ? (What's your name?)

Take It Further

In these sections, we'll expand on what you've seen so far.

We might break down some of the new phrases or sentences that you've seen, look more closely at additional words that were introduced, or expand on some of the grammar points.

For example, let's break down **Comment vas-tu ?**, **Comment allez-vous ?**, and **Ça va** from Vocabulary Builder 1:

comment	koh-mah(n)	how
ça (before a vowel, ça changes to c')	sah	it, that, this
ça va	sah vah	it goes
tu vas	tew vah	you go (familiar)
vous allez	voo zah-lay	you go (polite)

As you can see, French often uses forms of *to go* in greetings, similar to *How's it going?* or *It's going fine* in English.

Comment allez-vous ?/Comment vas-tu ?
How are you? (literally, How are you going?)

Ça va.
I'm fine. (literally, It's going./It goes.)

You'll learn more about *to go* in Lesson 8. Are you wondering why the order of **tu vas** and **vous allez** is reversed in those questions? That's actually just one way of forming a question in French. You'll learn more in Lesson 6.

2 Introduce yourself
Respond when people ask *How are you?*

Vocabulary Builder 2

▶ 1D Vocabulary Builder 2 (CD 1, Track 4)

Good evening.	**Bonsoir.**	boh(n)-swahr
How's it going? (How are you?)	**Comment ça va ?***	koh-mah(n) sah vah
It's going well.	**Ça va bien.**	sah vah bya(n)
It's not going well. (It's going badly.)	**Ça va mal.**	sah vah mahl
Not bad.	**Pas mal.**	pah mahl
So-so. (literally, Like this, like that.)	**Comme ci, comme ça.**	kohm see, kohm sah
Super.	**Super.**	sew-pehr
Fantastic.	**Formidable.**	fohr-mee-dah-bluh
My name is ... (literally, I am called ...)	**Je m'appelle...**	zhuh mah-pehl

* In casual conversation, you will often just hear **Ça va ?** [sah vah]

Pleased to meet you./ Nice to meet you.	Enchanté. (said by a man)/ Enchantée. (said by a woman)	ah(n)-shah(n)-tay/ ah(n)-shah(n)-tay

✎ Vocabulary Practice 2

Just like in Vocabulary Practice 1, fill in the blanks with the correct French translations.

Good evening. _____

How's it going?/How are you? _____

It's going well. _____

It's not going well./It's going badly. _____

Not bad. _____

So-so. _____

Super. _____

Fantastic. _____

My name is .../I am called ... _____

Pleased to meet you./Nice to meet you. _____

ANSWER KEY:
Bonsoir. (*Good evening.*); Comment ça va? (*How's it going?/How are you?*); Ça va bien. (*It's going well.*); Ça va mal. (*It's not going well./It's going badly.*); Pas mal. (*Not bad.*); Comme ci, comme ça. (*So-so.*); Super. (*Super.*); Formidable. (*Fantastic.*); Je m'appelle... (*My name is .../I am called ...*); Enchanté./Enchantée. (*Pleased to meet you./Nice to meet you.*)

Grammar Builder 2

Let's pause there for a moment, and review some of what you've learned—
but this time, let's translate from French into English. How many of the following
words and phrases do you know without going back to review? Fill in as many of
the English translations as you can in the corresponding blank spaces.

Once you're done, you'll have a handy review sheet for the key phrases in
this lesson!

▶ 1E Grammar Builder 2 (CD 1, Track 5). Listen to the audio to practice your pronunciation
of the phrases below! The audio also includes some English translations, so try to fill in
the blanks below first before you listen.

Greetings

Bonjour.	
Salut.	
Bonsoir.	

Formal (vous)

Comment allez-vous ?	
Comment vous appelez-vous ?	

Informal (tu)

Comment vas-tu ?	
Comment t'appelles-tu ?	

Question and Answer

Comment ça va ?	
Ça va bien.	
Ça va mal.	

Pas mal.	
Comme ci, comme ça.	
Super.	
Formidable.	

And finally:

Je m'appelle...	
Enchanté./Enchantée.	

Take It Further

Now that you can introduce yourself with **je m'appelle**, let's look at how to introduce other people.

tu t'appelles	tew tah-pehl	*you are called, your name is (familiar)*
vous vous appelez	voo voo zah-play	*you are called, your name is (polite)*

Tu t'appelles Jean.
tew tah-pehl zhah(n)
Your name is Jean./You're called Jean.

Vous vous appelez Marie.
voo voo zah-play mah-ree
Your name is Marie./You're called Marie.

Notice the similarity to **Comment t'appelles-tu ?/Comment vous appelez-vous ?** (*What's your name?*)? They are, in fact, the same phrases, just re-ordered to form a question. Again, you'll learn more about forming questions in Lesson 6.

Finally, let's look at some of the new individual words you saw in Vocabulary Builder 2:

je (before a vowel, je changes to j')	zhuh	*I*
bien	bya(n)	*well, fine, good*
mal	mahl	*badly, bad, wrong*
pas	pah	*not*
comme	kohm	*like, as, how*
ci	see	*this, here*

Although **pas** can be used on its own to mean *not*, you will more often see the phrase **ne... pas** [nuh ... pah] used to mean *not* or to negate a sentence. You'll see an example of **ne... pas** in use at the end of this lesson.

✎ Work Out 1

Okay, let's put everything you've learned so far together in a short comprehension exercise. Fill in the blanks in the conversation below.

▶ 1F Work Out 1 (CD 1, Track 6). Listen to the audio to practice pronouncing the following phrases. The audio also includes the French translations, so try to complete the exercise here first before listening.

_____, **comment allez-vous ?**

***Hello ma'am**, how are you?*

_____ , **merci.**

***Not bad**, thank you.*

_____ **François.**

***My name is** François.*

Je vous présente ma femme, Marguerite.

Let me introduce my wife, Marguerite.

_____ .

Pleased to meet you. *(said by a woman)*

_____ ?

What's your name? *(polite)*

_____ Madame Beaulieu.

My name is Mrs. Beaulieu.

Je vous présente mon mari, Monsieur Albert Beaulieu.

Let me introduce my husband, Mr. Albert Beaulieu.

_____ .

Pleased to meet you. *(said by a man)*

ANSWER KEY:
Bonjour madame; Pas mal; Je m'appelle; Enchantée; Comment vous appelez-vous; Je m'appelle; Enchanté

Take It Further

Notice some new vocabulary? Here are some of the new phrases that you saw:

merci	mehr-see	*thank you*
Je vous présente...	zhuh voo pray-zah(n)t	*Let me introduce ... (literally, I introduce to you ...) (polite)*
ma femme	mah fahm	*my wife*
mon mari	moh(n) mah-ree	*my husband*

You'll learn more about **mon** [moh(n)] and **ma** [mah], which both mean *my*, in Lesson 5.

---

3 Use what you've learned when meeting people for the first time

◖ Bring It All Together

Now let's bring it all together and add a little bit more vocabulary and structure. Read and listen to the following short dialogue.

▶ 1G Bring It All Together (CD 1, Track 7)

A: *Hi, I'm Mark, what's your name?*
Salut, je suis Marc, comment t'appelles-tu ?
sah-lew, zhuh swee mahrk, koh-mah(n) tah-pehl-tew

B: *Hi, Mark, my name is Stephanie.*
Salut, Marc, je m'appelle Stéphanie.
sah-lew, mahrk, zhuh mah-pehl stay-fah-nee

A: *Nice to meet you. How's it going?*
Enchanté. Comment ça va ?
ah(n)-shah(n)-tay. koh-mah(n) sah vah

B: *Super!*
Super !
sew-pehr

A: *Let me introduce my father.*

Je te présente mon père.

zhuh tuh pray-zah(n)t moh(n) pehr

B: *Hello, sir. How are you?*

Bonjour monsieur. Comment allez-vous ?

boh(n)-zhoor, muh-syuh. koh-mah(n) tah-lay-voo

C: *I'm very well, thank you.*

Je vais très bien, merci.

zhuh veh treh bya(n), mehr-see

A: *Bye, Stephanie!*

Salut, Stéphanie !

sah-lew, stay-fah-nee

B: *Bye, Mark!*

Salut, Marc !

sah-lew, mahrk

Take It Further

1H Take It Further (CD 1, Track 8)

Okay, you already knew a lot of that vocabulary, but there were a few new words too.

Did you notice that you can introduce yourself by simply saying:

je suis	zhuh swee	I am

Say that again: je suis... je suis... je suis... Good!

And to introduce someone else, you can say:

Je te présente...	zhuh tuh pray-zah(n)t	Let me introduce ... (if you're speaking to a friend or family member)
Je vous présente...	zhuh voo pray-zah(n)t	Let me introduce ... (if you're speaking more formally)

(Remember je vous présente from Work Out 1? Now you know the familiar form: je te présente.)

Other helpful words and phrases from Bring It All Together include:

Je vais très bien.	zhuh veh treh bya(n)	I'm very well. (literally, I go very well.)
je vais	zhuh veh	I go
très	treh	very
père	pehr	father

You'll learn more family terms in the next lesson.

✎ Work Out 2

Now let's practice some of what you've learned.

▶ 1I Work Out 2 (CD 1, Track 9) for a different, audio-only exercise!

Can you find the French translations of the English phrases in the puzzle below?

1. *I am*

2. *Good evening*

3. *Hi*

4. *I'm fine*

5. *ma'am*

J	B	O	N	S	O	I	R
Ç	E	N	T	É	S	A	C
L	S	S	A	L	U	T	I
M	E	N	U	E	S	O	Ç
A	N	T	É	I	R	I	A
R	T	Ç	V	E	S	U	V
E	M	A	D	A	M	E	A
D	E	D	J	O	S	L	L

ANSWER KEY:
1. **Je suis** (*I am*); 2. **Bonsoir** (*Good evening*); 3. **Salut** (*Hi*); 4. **Ça va** (*I'm fine*); 5. madame (*ma'am*)

✎ Drive It Home

Let's do one more practice before the end of the lesson.

This exercise is designed to ingrain key information about French structure. Although it may seem repetitive, it is *very* important that you read through each question carefully, write out each response, and then read the whole question aloud. It will help you to retain the information beyond just this lesson and course.

A. First let's practice the familiar *you*. Fill in each blank with tu. Then, read each sentence aloud. Ready?

1. _____ vas *you go*

2. Comment t'appelles- _____ ? *What is your name?*

3. _____ t'appelles Isabelle. *Your name is Isabelle.*

4. Comment vas- _____ ? *How are you?*

B. Now let's practice the polite *you*. Fill in each blank with vous, and don't forget to read each sentence aloud.

1. Comment allez- _____ ? *How are you?*

2. _____ allez *you go*

3. Comment _____ appelez-_____ ? *What is your name?*

4. _____ appelez Florian. *Your name is Florian.*

ANSWER KEY:
A: all tu
B: all vous (there are two vous in 4)

Parting Words

Congratulations!

Félicitations !

fay-lee-see-tah-syoh(n)

You've finished the lesson! How did you do? You should now be able to:

☐ Greet someone and ask how they're doing (Still unsure? Go back to page 11)

☐ Address someone formally and informally (Still unsure? Go back to page 13)

☐ Introduce yourself (Still unsure? Go back to page 15)

☐ Respond when people ask *How are you?* (Still unsure? Go back to page 15)

☐ Use what you've learned when meeting people for the first time (Still unsure? Go back to page 21)

Take It Further

▶ 1K Take It Further (CD 1, Track 11)

Some other key phrases you might want to know are:

Comment ?*	koh-mah(n)	*Pardon?/* *What did you say?*
Répétez, s'il vous plaît.	ray-pay-tay, seel voo pleh	*Repeat (that), please.*
Parlez plus lentement, s'il vous plaît.	pahr-lay plew lah(n)t- mah(n), seel voo pleh	*Speak more slowly, please.*
Je ne comprends pas.	zhuh nuh koh(m)-prah(n) pah	*I don't understand.*

* Remember that **comment** also means *how*.

** Notice the use of **ne... pas** here to mean *not*.

| J'apprends le français. | zhah-prah(n) luh frah(n)-seh | *I'm learning French.* |
| Je parle un peu français. | zhuh pahrl uh(n) puh frah(n)-seh | *I speak a little French.* |

Those few phrases are important for beginners of français [frah(n)-seh] (*French*) to know, so practice them a few times, s'il vous plaît [seel voo pleh] (*please*)!

In the next lesson, we'll learn how to talk about the family, but if you'd like to review Lesson 1 first, go right ahead! You can learn at your own pace.

Don't forget to go to *www.livinglanguage.com/languagelab* to access your free online tools for this lesson: flashcards, games, and quizzes.

Word Recall

You will see a Word Recall section in between lessons. Word Recalls review important vocabulary and grammar from any of the previous lessons, including the one you just finished. They reinforce what you've learned so far in the course, and help you remember the information for the long term.

Of course, since we're currently at the end of the first lesson, we'll only review key vocabulary and grammar from Lesson 1 here.

A. Match the French phrases on the left to the English translations on the right.

1. bonjour	a. *hi*
2. au revoir	b. *good-bye*
3. merci	c. *good evening*
4. s'il vous plaît	d. *hello*
5. enchanté	e. *please*
6. salut	f. *nice to meet you/pleased to meet you*
7. bonsoir	g. *thank you*

ANSWER KEY:
1. d; 2. b.; 3. g.; 4. e.; 5. f.; 6. a.; 7. c

Lesson 2: People and the Family

Leçon deux : les gens et la famille

luh-soh(n) duh: lay zhah(n) ay lah fah-meey

Bienvenue ! [bya(n)-vuh-new] *Welcome!* In this lesson, you'll learn how to talk about your family, and you'll learn some key vocabulary related to people in general. At the same time, you'll learn some of the basics of French grammar to get you speaking right away.

You will learn how to:

1 Talk about people
Use *a/an* in French

2 Talk about your family
Use *the* in French

3 Use what you've learned to tell someone about your family

But first, let's get started with some vocabulary. Prête, madame ? [preht, mah-dahm] *Ready, ma'am?* Prêt, monsieur ? [preh, muh-syuh] *Ready, sir?*

Remember to look for these symbols, ▶ and ⏸, to help guide you through the audio as you're reading the book. If you don't see ▶, then there isn't any audio for that section.

1 Talk about people
Use *a/an* in French

Vocabulary Builder 1

▶ 2B Vocabulary Builder 1 (CD 1, Track 13)

a person	**une personne**	ewn pehr-sohn
a woman	**une femme***	ewn fahm
This is ...	**C'est...**	seh
This is a woman.	**C'est une femme.**	seh tewn fahm
a man	**un homme**	uh(n) nohm
This is a man.	**C'est un homme.**	seh tuh(n) nohm
a girl	**une fille***	ewn feey
This is a girl.	**C'est une fille.**	seh tewn feey
a boy	**un garçon**	uh(n) gahr-soh(n)
This is a boy.	**C'est un garçon.**	seh tuh(n) gahr-soh(n)
a child	**un enfant**	uh(n) nah(n)-fah(n)
This is a child.	**C'est un enfant.**	seh tuh(n) nah(n)-fah(n)

* As you saw in Lesson 1, **femme** can also mean *wife*.

⏸ ** **Fille** can also mean *daughter*, as you'll see in Vocabulary Builder 2.

✎ Vocabulary Practice 1

Time to practice! As always, fill in the blanks with the correct French translations.

This is ... _____

a person _____

*a woman, a wife*_____

a man _____

*a girl, a daughter*_____

a boy _____

*a child*_____

ANSWER KEY:
C'est... (*This is ...*); une personne (*a person*); une femme (*a woman, a wife*); un homme (*a man*); une fille (*a girl, a daughter*); un garçon (*a boy*); un enfant (*a child*)

Grammar Builder 1

▶ 2C Grammar Builder 1 (CD 1, Track 14)

Okay, let's stop there.

You learned how to say:

a person	une personne
a woman	une femme
a man	un homme
a girl	une fille
a boy	un garçon
a child	un enfant

Did you notice that there are two words for *a*, either un [uh(n)] or une [ewn]? That's because French nouns are all either masculine or feminine.

The feminine form of *a* (or *an*), also known as the "indefinite article," is une.

une femme	*a woman*
une fille	*a girl*

The masculine form of the indefinite article is **un**.

un homme	*a man*
un garçon	*a boy*

It's easy to remember the gender of nouns like *man, woman, girl,* or *boy,* but in French, all nouns have gender. Sometimes it's not logical; *a person* is **une personne**, and *a child* is **un enfant**.

And often it's downright impossible; cars, tables, houses, trees, rocks, and all other nouns have gender. It's best not to overthink it! Just memorize the gender of each new noun you learn.

So, to summarize:

FEMININE	MASCULINE
une (*a/an*)	un (*a/an*)
une femme (*a woman*)	un homme (*a man*)

Take It Further

Note that the word **enfant** (*child*) can actually be masculine **or** feminine. It's masculine (**un enfant**) if you're using it as a general term for *child* (as in, *a child would love that toy*), or if you're referring specifically to a male *child*. However, if you're referring specifically to a female *child*, then it's feminine: **une enfant**.

2 Talk about your family
Use *the* in French

Vocabulary Builder 2

2D Vocabulary Builder 2 (CD 1, Track 15)

This is a family.	C'est une famille.	seh tewn fah-meey
Here is ...	Voilà...	vwah-lah
Here's the father.	Voilà le père.	vwah-lah luh pehr
Here's the mother.	Voilà la mère.	vwah-lah lah mehr
Here's the son.	Voilà le fils.	vwah-lah luh fees
Here's the daughter.	Voilà la fille.*	vwah-lah lah feey
Here's the brother.	Voilà le frère.	vwah-lah luh frehr
Here's the sister.	Voilà la sœur.	vwah-lah lah suhr

* Remember that fille can also mean *girl*.

Vocabulary Practice 2

Just like in Vocabulary Practice 1, fill in blanks with the correct French translations.

Note that sometimes you will need to do a bit of deciphering to fill in these Vocabulary Practices—looking up words in a dictionary, breaking down a sentence on your own, and so on. This is meant to help you think more carefully and more in detail about the sentences that you're seeing, and to mimic situations where you won't always understand each word.

If you're confused, always feel free to look up a word in the dictionary or the glossary, or simply check the Answer Key.

Here is ... _____

a family _____

the father _____

the mother _____

the son _____

the daughter, the girl _____

the brother _____

the sister _____

ANSWER KEY:
Voilà... (*Here is ...*); **une famille** (*a family*); **le père** (*the father*); **la mère** (*the mother*); **le fils** (*the son*); **la fille** (*the daughter, the girl*); **le frère** (*the brother*); **la sœur** (*the sister*)

Grammar Builder 2

▶ 2E Grammar Builder 2 (CD 1, Track 16)

Let's pause again.

First you learned how to say *a* (or *an*) in French: **un** for masculine nouns, and **une** for feminine nouns.

Now you've just learned how to say *the*, also known as the "definite article." Again, gender is important. The masculine form is **le** [luh], and the feminine form is **la** [lah]. So far, you've learned a few feminine nouns:

FEMININE (LA)	
la famille	*the family*
la mère	*the mother*
la fille	*the daughter* or *the girl*

FEMININE (LA)	
la sœur	*the sister*
la personne	*the person*

And you've learned a few masculine nouns too:

MASCULINE (LE)	
le père	*the father*
le fils	*the son*
le garçon	*the boy*
le frère	*the brother*
l'homme	*the man*
l'enfant*	*the child*

* Remember that **enfant** (*child*) is masculine if you're using *child* in a general sense, or if you're talking about a male *child*. However, **enfant** is feminine if you're referring to a female *child*.

Notice in those last two words that **le** is shortened to just an **l'** before nouns that start with a vowel. The same thing happens to **la**.

So:

le (*the*) + **étudiant** (*male student*) = **l'étudiant** (*the male student*)

la (*the*) + **étudiante** (*female student*) = **l'étudiante** (*the female student*)

The same thing happens before many (but not all!) nouns that begin with **h**, such as **homme**, since **h** is silent in French.

Take It Further

In Vocabulary Builder 2, you saw the very useful word voilà.

Voilà means *here is* and *here are*, or *there is* and *there are*. Voilà can also be used on its own as an exclamation to mean *here it is!* and *here they are!*, or *there it is!* and *there they are!*.

A similar word is voici [vwah-see]. Voici can also be translated as *here is* and *here are*, and *here it is!* and *here they are!*.

So what's the difference between voici and voilà? Well, là [lah] on its own means *there*, while ci means *here*. So, technically, voici refers to something *here*, while voilà refers to something *there*. In other words, voici means *here is* and voilà means *there is*. However, in practice, voilà can also be used to mean *here is*, as you saw in this lesson.

✎ Work Out 1

Okay, let's put everything you've learned so far together in a short comprehension exercise.

▶ 2F Work Out 1 (CD 1, Track 17). Listen to the audio to practice your pronunciation of the phrases below. The audio also includes the English translations, so try to do the exercise below first before you listen.

Try to translate as much of the text below as you can, keeping in mind that est [eh] means *is*. You'll learn more about est in the next Take It Further.

C'est la famille Lacroix. Madame Lacroix est une femme. Monsieur Lacroix est un homme. Marc est un garçon. Sophie est une fille.

Madame Lacroix est la mère. Monsieur Lacroix est le père. Sophie est la fille. Marc est le fils.

———————————————————————————————

———————————————————————————————

———————————————————————————————

———————————————————————————————

———————————————————————————————

———————————————————————————————

———————————————————————————————

ANSWER KEY:

This is the Lacroix family. Mrs. Lacroix is a woman. Mr. Lacroix is a man. Marc is a boy. Sophie is a girl. Mrs. Lacroix is the mother. Mr. Lacroix is the father. Sophie is the daughter. Marc is the son.

3 Use what you've learned to tell someone about your family

ᴳ Bring It All Together

Now let's bring it all together and add a little bit more vocabulary and structure. Read and listen to the following short monologue about Mark and his family.

▶ 2G Bring It All Together (CD 1, Track 18)

Hello!

Bonjour !

boh(n)-zhoor

Lesson 2: People and the Family   37

I'm Marc.
Je suis Marc.
zhuh swee mahrk

I'm French.
Je suis français.
zhuh swee frah(n)-seh

I have a small family.
J'ai une petite famille.
zheh ewn puh-teet fah-meey

I have a father ...
J'ai un père...
zheh uh(n) pehr

He's a policeman.
Il est policier.
eel eh poh-lee-syay

And I have a mother ...
Et j'ai une mère...
ay zheh ewn mehr

She's a teacher.
Elle est professeure.
ehl eh proh-fay-suhr

And I have a sister.
Et j'ai une sœur.
ay zheh ewn suhr

She's a student.
Elle est étudiante.
ehl eh tay-tew-dyah(n)t

And me, too, I'm a student.
Et moi aussi, je suis étudiant.
ay mwah oh-see, zhuh swee ay-tew-dyah(n)

Take It Further

2H Take It Further (CD 1, Track 19)

Okay, you already knew a lot of that vocabulary, but there were a few new words, too.

You already know that **bonjour** [boh(n)-zhoor] means *hello* and **français** [frah(n)-seh] means *French* (both the language and the nationality!).

Did you remember that **je suis** [zhuh swee] means *I am*? You also learned two other forms:

il est	eel eh	he is
elle est	ehl eh	she is

You'll learn more about that useful verb (*to be*) later.

And speaking of useful verbs, you also saw Marc say **j'ai** [zheh], meaning *I have*, as in **j'ai une petite famille** [zheh ewn puh-teet fah-meey], or *I have a small family.* Repeat that: **j'ai… j'ai… j'ai…**

Finally, you saw Marc say:

un policier	uh(n) poh-lee-syay	*a policeman*
une professeure	ewn proh-fay-suhr	*a (female) teacher*
une étudiante	ewn ay-tew-dyah(n)t	*a (female) student*
un étudiant	uh(n) nay-tew-dyah(n)	*a (male) student*

(Remember étudiant/étudiante from earlier in the lesson?)

As an additional note, here is some more helpful vocabulary from Bring It All Together:

petit/petite	puh-tee/puh-teet	*small, little, short*
et	ay	*and*
aussi	oh-see	*also, too*
moi	mwah	*me*

Wondering why there are two different ways to say *small* in French (petit and petite)? You'll find out more in Lesson 5.

If you're also wondering why you don't use un (*a/an*) in il est policier (*he is a policeman*), it's actually due to a rule in French. In general, French doesn't use articles like *a/an* in front of professions. For example, as you can see in Bring It All Together, you also say elle est professeure, elle est étudiante, and je suis étudiant (you would **not** say elle est une professeure, etc.).

You'll learn more about professions in Lesson 9.

✎ Work Out 2

Now let's practice some of what you've learned.

▶ 2I Work Out 2 (CD 1, Track 20) for different, audio-only exercises!

A. J'ai... *I have* ... Fill in the blanks using **un** or **une**.

1. _____ père.

2. _____ sœur.

3. _____ mère.

4. _____ fils.

5. _____ famille.

B. Je suis... *I am* ... Match the professions to the correct English translations.

1. étudiante	a. *male student*
2. professeure	b. *policeman*
3. étudiant	c. *female teacher*
4. policier	d. *female student*

ANSWER KEY:

⏸ A: 1. un; 2. une; 3. une; 4. un; 5. une
B: 1. d; 2. c; 3. a; 4. b

✎ Drive It Home

Now let's do one final practice of the grammar you learned in this lesson. As we mentioned in Lesson 1, although this exercise may seem repetitive, it is **very** important that you complete each question carefully and then say it out loud. It will help you to retain the information for the long term.

A. Fill in the blanks with le (or l') and then read each French sentence aloud. Ready?

1. _____ homme est étudiant. (*The man is a student.*)

2. _____ frère est étudiant. (*The brother is a student.*)

3. _____ père est étudiant. (*The father is a student.*)

4. _____ fils est étudiant. (*The son is a student.*)

5. _____ garçon est étudiant. (*The boy is a student.*)

6. _____ mari est étudiant. (*The husband is a student.*)

B. Great. Now do the same thing, but this time with la (or l').

1. _____ fille est étudiante. (*The girl/daughter is a student.*)

2. _____ femme est étudiante. (*The woman/wife is a student.*)

3. _____ sœur est étudiante. (*The sister is a student.*)

4. _____ personne est étudiante. (*The person is a student.*)

5. _____ mère est étudiante. (*The mother is a student.*)

ANSWER KEY:
A: 1 is l' and the rest are le
B: all la

Parting Words

Congratulations!

Félicitations !

fay-lee-see-tah-syoh(n)

You've finished the lesson! How did you do? You should now be able to:

☐ Talk about people (Still unsure? Go back to page 30)

☐ Use *a/an* in French (Still unsure? Go back to page 31)

☐ Talk about your family (Still unsure? Go back to page 33)

☐ Use *the* in French (Still unsure? Go back to page 34)

☐ Use what you've learned to tell someone about your family
(Still unsure? Go back to page 37)

Take It Further

▶ 2K Take It Further (CD 1, Track 22)

You may of course want to extend the discussion a bit, and talk about:

an uncle	**un oncle**	uh(n) noh(n)k-luh
an aunt	**une tante**	ewn tah(n)t
a female cousin	**une cousine**	ewn koo-zeen
a male cousin	**un cousin**	uh(n) koo-za(n)

And what family reunion would be complete without:

| *a grandmother* | **une grand-mère** | ewn grah(n)-mehr |
| *a grandfather* | **un grand-père** | uh(n) grah(n)-pehr |

(Or, more generally, **un grand-parent** [uh(n) grah(n)-pah-rah(n)], *a grandparent.*)

If you're **un oncle** or **une tante**, that means you must have:

| *a nephew* | **un neveu** | uh(n) nuh-vuh |
| *a niece* | **une nièce** | ewn neeyehs |

Now, do you remember your survival phrases from Lesson 1? Here they are again:

Comment ?	koh-mah(n)	*Pardon?/* *What did you say?*
Répétez, s'il vous plaît.	ray-pay-tay, seel voo pleh	*Repeat (that), please.*
Parlez plus lentement, s'il vous plaît.	pahr-lay plew lah(n)t-mah(n), seel voo pleh	*Speak more slowly, please.*
Je ne comprends pas.	zhuh nuh koh(m)-prah(n) pah	*I don't understand.*
J'apprends le français.	zhah-prah(n) luh frah(n)-seh	*I'm learning French.*
Je parle un peu français.	zhuh pahrl uh(n) puh frah(n)-seh	*I speak a little French.*

See that, you're learning more and more!

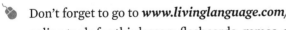

Don't forget to go to *www.livinglanguage.com/languagelab* to access your free online tools for this lesson: flashcards, games, and quizzes.

Word Recall

Let's review family vocabulary. Fill in the following family tree with the correct French word for each member of the family. Make sure to include **le** or **la** before each French word.

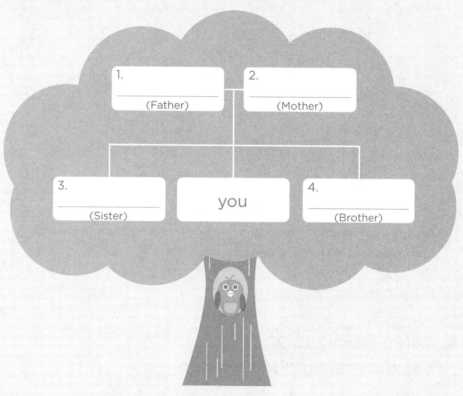

1. _____ (Father)

2. _____ (Mother)

3. _____ (Sister)

you

4. _____ (Brother)

ANSWER KEY:
1. **le père** (*the father*); 2. **la mère** (*the mother*); 3. **la sœur** (*the sister*); 4. **le frère** (*the brother*)

Lesson 3: Numbers

Leçon trois : les nombres
luh-soh(n) trwah: lay noh(m)-bruh

Déjà plus de français ? [day-zhah plews duh frah(n)-seh] *More French already?*
Mais, bien sûr ! [meh, bya(n) sewr] *But, of course!*

In this lesson, you'll learn how to:

1 Count from 1 to 22
Say *the men* and *the women*

2 Count from 22 to 1,000
Say *I am, you are,* etc.

3 Use what you've learned to describe a photograph

Allons-y ! [ah-loh(n)-zee] *Let's go!*

1 Count from 1 to 22
Say *the men* and *the women*

Vocabulary Builder 1

It helps to learn numbers in groups, so we'll count in sets of two or three. Note that *zero* in French is just **zéro** [zay-roh].

▶ 3B Vocabulary Builder 1 (CD 1, Track 24)

one, two, three	un*, deux, trois	uh(n), duh, trwah
four, five, six	quatre, cinq, six	kah-truh, sa(n)k, sees
seven, eight	sept, huit	seht, weet
nine, ten	neuf, dix	nuhf, dees
eleven, twelve, thirteen	onze, douze, treize	oh(n)z, dooz, trehz
fourteen, fifteen, sixteen	quatorze, quinze, seize	kah-tohrz, ka(n)z, sehz
seventeen, eighteen, nineteen	dix-sept, dix-huit, dix-neuf	dees-seht, dee-zweet, deez-nuhf
twenty, twenty-one, twenty-two	vingt, vingt et un, vingt-deux	va(n), va(n)-tay-uh(n), va(n)t-duh

* **Un** (*one*) is used when counting (*one, two, three, four ...*), or before a masculine noun. Before a feminine noun, however, you would use **une** (*one*). Remember that **un/une** also means *a* or *an*, so now you know that **un/une** can actually mean *a, an,* or *one*: **une personne** (*one person, a person*), **un homme** (*one man, a man*), and so on.

✏ Vocabulary Practice 1

Now let's practice the numbers you just learned. As always, fill in the blanks with the correct French translations.

zero _____

one _____

two_____

three _____

four _____

five_____

six _____

seven _____

eight _____

nine _____

ten _____

eleven _____

twelve _____

thirteen _____

fourteen _____

fifteen _____

sixteen _____

seventeen _____

eighteen _____

nineteen _____

twenty _____

twenty-one _____

twenty-two _____

ANSWER KEY:

zéro (zero); un/une (one); deux (two); trois (three); quatre (four); cinq (five); six (six); sept (seven); huit (eight); neuf (nine); dix (ten); onze (eleven); douze (twelve); treize (thirteen); quatorze (fourteen); quinze (fifteen); seize (sixteen); dix-sept (seventeen); dix-huit (eighteen); dix-neuf (nineteen); vingt (twenty); vingt et un (twenty-one); vingt-deux (twenty-two)

Grammar Builder 1

▶ 3C Grammar Builder 1 (CD 1, Track 25)

Now let's use some of those numbers to count things, which means using the plural form of nouns.

Plurals in French are usually written with an -s, but they sound just like the singular because the -s is (generally) silent. You can tell the difference (if you're unsure while listening to someone speak) because the plural noun comes with the plural form of *the*, which is les [lay], or a phrase like beaucoup de [boh-koo duh] (*a lot of, many*), or a number.

(In other words, it's easy to tell whether a noun is plural in writing because you can just look to see if it has an -s at the end of it. However, when listening to someone speak, you usually can't *hear* the difference, and that's where words like les, beaucoup de, and numbers can help let you know that the noun is plural.)

Here are some examples:

people (*literally, the people*)	les gens	lay zhah(n)
men and women (*literally, the men and the women*)	les hommes et les femmes	lay zohm ay lay fahm
one man and three boys	un homme et trois garçons	uh(n) nohm ay trwah gahr-soh(n)
two women and five girls	deux femmes et cinq filles	duh fahm ay sa(n)k feey
many families	beaucoup de familles	boh-koo duh fah-meey

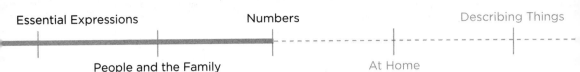
So, even if a noun sounds the same in the singular and plural, if you hear it with a number, with les, or with beaucoup de, you know it's plural.

Okay, you just learned two key grammar points, so let's summarize.

1. The plural in French is usually formed by adding a silent -s to the end of a word. For example:

| la femme | lah fahm | *the woman* |
| les femmes | lay fahm | *the women* |

2. Les is the plural *the*. It can be used with both masculine and feminine plural nouns.

Take It Further

Note that French uses articles like le, la, and les a lot more than English does, so you don't always translate them. In fact, French nouns are almost always preceded by something, whether it's an article (le, la, les, un, une), a number, a phrase like beaucoup de (which, by the way, becomes beaucoup d' before a vowel), and so on. For example, French speakers would never just say *Books are inexpensive*. They would say *The books are inexpensive*. You'll see examples of this throughout the course.

2 Count from 22 to 1,000
Say *I am, you are,* etc.

Vocabulary Builder 2

▶ 3D Vocabulary Builder 2 (CD 1, Track 26)

Now let's add some more numbers.

The numbers **vingt-deux** [va(n)t-duh] (*twenty-two*) through **soixante-neuf** [swah-sah(n)t-nuhf] (*sixty-nine*) work a lot like in English. Just put the ones place (such as **deux**, *two*) after the tens place (such as **vingt**, *twenty*).

If the ones place is **un**, say the phrase **et un** [ay uh(n)] (*and one*), as in **trente et un** [trah(n)t ay uh(n)] (*thirty-one*). (Or literally, *thirty and one.*)

thirty, thirty-one, thirty-five	**trente, trente et un, trente-cinq**	trah(n)t, trah(n)t ay uh(n), trah(n)t-sa(n)k
forty, fifty, sixty-six	**quarante, cinquante, soixante-six**	kah-rah(n)t, sa(n)-kah(n)t, swah-sah(n)t-sees

Seventy through *ninety-nine* involve a little math:

seventy (*literally, sixty-ten*)	**soixante-dix**	swah-sah(n)t-dees
seventy-one (*literally, sixty and eleven*)	**soixante et onze**	swah-sah(n)t ay oh(n)z
eighty (*literally, four-twenties*)	**quatre-vingts**	kah-truh-va(n)
ninety (*literally, four-twenty-ten*)	**quatre-vingt-dix**	kah-truh-va(n)-dees

ninety-one (*literally, four-twenty-eleven*)	**quatre-vingt-onze**	kah-truh-va(n)-oh(n)z

Notice that the et (*and*) is dropped in quatre-vingt-onze, unlike in *seventy-one*: soixante et onze.

Here are more examples:

seventy, seventy-five, seventy-nine	**soixante-dix, soixante-quinze, soixante-dix-neuf**	swah-sah(n)t-dees, swah-sah(n)t-ka(n)z, swah-sah(n)t-deez-nuhf
eighty, eighty-five, ninety	**quatre-vingts, quatre-vingt-cinq, quatre-vingt-dix***	kah-truh-va(n), kah-truh-va(n)-sa(n)k, kah-truh-va(n)-dees
one hundred, one thousand	**cent, mille**	sah(n), meel

* Note that quatre-vingts loses its final -s when it's followed by a number: quatre-vingt-cinq, quatre-vingt-dix.

✎ Vocabulary Practice 2

The higher numbers in French can be a bit confusing—there's even some math involved! However, the best thing to do is simply practice.

So with that in mind, fill in the blanks below with the correct French translations.

thirty _____   *fifty* _____

thirty-one _____   *sixty* _____

thirty-five _____   *seventy* _____

forty _____   *seventy-one* _____

seventy-five _____   *ninety-one* _____

eighty _____   *one hundred* _____

eighty-five _____   *one thousand* _____

ninety _____

ANSWER KEY:

trente (*thirty*); **trente et un** (*thirty-one*); **trente-cinq** (*thirty-five*); **quarante** (*forty*); **cinquante** (*fifty*); **soixante** (*sixty*); **soixante-dix** (*seventy*); **soixante et onze** (*seventy-one*); **soixante-quinze** (*seventy-five*); **quatre-vingts** (*eighty*); **quatre-vingt-cinq** (*eighty-five*); **quatre-vingt-dix** (*ninety*); **quatre-vingt-onze** (*ninety-one*); **cent** (*one hundred*); **mille** (*one thousand*)

Grammar Builder 2

▶ 3E Grammar Builder 2 (CD 1, Track 27)

Now let's look at pronouns (*I, you, he, she,* etc.) and **être** [eh-truh], or *to be.*

You've already seen a few forms, but let's look at the whole conjugation:

ÊTRE *(TO BE)*		
I am	**je suis**	zhuh swee
you are (familiar)	**tu es**	tew eh
he is, she is	**il est, elle est**	eel eh, ehl eh
we are	**nous sommes**	noo sohm
you are (polite/plural)	**vous êtes**	voo zeht
they are	**ils sont, elles sont**	eel soh(n), ehl soh(n)

Don't forget that in French there are two ways to say *you.* **Tu es** is the familiar *you are,* so you'd use it with your friends, family, or anyone you're close to. **Vous êtes** is more polite, ***and*** it is also used to refer to groups of people, as in *all of you are.*

Also note that there are two forms of *they are*:

Masculine/Mixed*	ils sont
Feminine	elles sont

* In other words, you would use it to refer to a group of men or to a mixed group of men and women.

Another common pronoun in French is **on** [oh(n)], which means *people in general,* but which also is ***often*** used to mean *we* (mainly in casual conversation). So, **on est** [oh(n) neh] can mean the same thing as **nous sommes.**

(Notice that **on** uses the same form as **il** and **elle**. You say **il est, elle est,** and **on est.**)

Take It Further

That was a good amount of information, so before continuing on, let's review.

Here are all of the French "subject pronouns" you just learned, with some additional detail provided. Subject pronouns are words like *I, you, he, she,* etc.

je (j')	zhuh	*I*
tu	tew	*you (familiar)*
il	eel	*he, it (masculine)*
elle	ehl	*she, it (feminine)*
on	oh(n)	*we (familiar), people in general, one*
nous	noo	*we*
vous	voo	*you (polite/plural)*
ils	eel	*they (masculine/mixed)*
elles	ehl	*they (feminine)*

Notice that **on** can also mean *one*, as in: *How does one get to the post office?*

In addition, it's important to reiterate that **vous** is the polite *you **and*** the plural *you* (familiar or polite). In other words, you would use **vous** to address your boss, but also a group of friends.

Furthermore, notice that **il** and **elle** can also mean *it*. So, **il est/elle est** can mean *he is/she is* or *it is.*

Il est petit.
eel eh puh-tee
It is little./He is little.

You would use **il** to mean *it* when referring to a masculine noun, and **elle** to mean *it* when referring to a feminine noun.

Also keep in mind that subject pronouns (**je, tu, il, elle**, etc.) ***replace*** nouns. For example, instead of **Marie**, you say **elle** (*she*). Consequently, you would use the same form of the verb for **Marie** that you would for **elle**:

Marie est étudiante. Elle est étudiante.
mah-ree eh tay-tew-dyah(n)t. ehl eh tay-tew-dyah(n)t.
Marie is a student. She is a student.

Here are a few more examples:

Paul et Marie sont étudiants. Ils sont étudiants.
pohl ay mah-ree soh(n) tay-tew-dyah(n). eel soh(n) tay-tew-dyah(n)
Paul and Marie are students. They are students.

Lesson 3: Numbers   55

Paul et moi sommes étudiants. Nous sommes étudiants.

pohl ay mwah sohm zay-tew-dyah(n). noo sohm zay-tew-dyah(n)

Paul and I are students (literally, Paul and me are students). We are students.

Le T-shirt est petit. Il est petit.

luh tee-shehrt eh puh-tee. eel eh puh-tee

The t-shirt is little. It is little.

✎ Work Out 1

Let's put everything you've learned so far together in a short comprehension exercise. Fill in the blanks in the sentences below.

▶ 3F Work Out 1 (CD 1, Track 28). Listen to the audio to practice pronouncing the following sentences! The audio also includes the French translations, so try to complete the exercise here first before listening.

1. **Amélie** _____ **, et Franck** _____

   _____ **amis.**

   *Amélie **is a girl**, and Franck **is a boy**. **They are** friends.*

2. **Êtes-vous américains ou français ?** _____ **suisses.**

   *Are you American or French? **We are** Swiss.*

3. _____ **?** _____ **ici.**

   ***The (male) students? They are** here.*

4. _____ **et** _____ **là-bas.**

   The women** and ***the men are over there.*

ANSWER KEY:
1. est une fille, est un garçon, Ils sont; 2. Nous sommes/On est; 3. Les étudiants, Ils sont; 4. Les femmes, les hommes sont

Take It Further

You saw some new vocabulary in that exercise:

ou	oo	or
l'ami/l'amie	lah-mee/lah-mee	*male friend/female friend*
américain/américaine (américains is simply the plural form of américain)	ah-may-ree-ka(n)/ ah-may-ree-kehn	*American*
suisse (suisses is simply the plural form of suisse)	swees	*Swiss*
ici	ee-see	*here*
là-bas	lah-bah	*over there*

Notice that *American* has two singular forms in French, but *Swiss* doesn't. You'll learn more in Lesson 5.

Finally, you learned earlier in this lesson that the pronoun ils is used for both masculine and mixed company. Well, masculine plural nouns work the same way. In other words, you would use les étudiants to refer to a group of male students or to a mixed group of male and female students. However, les étudiantes can only refer to a group of female students.

Similarly, you would use les amis to refer to a group of male friends or to a mixed group of male and female friends, while les amies can only refer to a group of female friends.

3 Use what you've learned to describe a photograph

Bring It All Together

Now let's bring it all together and add a little bit more vocabulary and structure.
Read and listen to the following dialogue between two friends looking at a photo.

▶ 3G Bring It All Together (CD 1, Track 29)

A: *It's a beautiful photo.*
C'est une belle photo.
seh tewn behl foh-toh

B: *There are six people.*
Il y a six personnes.
eel ee yah see pehr-sohn

A: *There are three men, two women, and a girl.*
Il y a trois hommes, deux femmes et une fille.
eel ee yah trwah zohm, duh fahm ay ewn feey

B: *Two men and one woman are standing.*
Deux hommes et une femme sont debout.
duh zohm ay ewn fahm soh(n) duh-boo

A: *And the others are sitting.*
Et les autres sont assis.
ay lay zoh-truh soh(n) tah-see

B: *There are also a lot of trees.*
Il y a aussi beaucoup d'arbres.
eel ee yah oh-see boh-koo dahr-bruh

⏸

Take It Further

Okay, you already knew a lot of that vocabulary, but there were a few new words, too.

Il y a...	eel ee yah	*There is .../There are ...*
beau/bel/belle	boh/behl/behl	*beautiful, handsome*
une photo	ewn foh-toh	*a photo*
un arbre	uh(n) nahr-bruh	*a tree*
autre	oh-truh	*other*
les autres	lay zoh-truh	*the others, the other ones*
debout	duh-boo	*standing*
assis/assise	ah-see/ah-seez	*sitting (down), seated*

Finally, as you saw in the dialogue, **c'est** can mean *it is* in addition to *this is*. It can also mean *that is*.

✎ Work Out 2

Now let's practice some of what you've learned.

▶ 3H Work Out 2 (CD 1, Track 30) for different, audio-only exercises! You'll also hear the helpful word **avec** [ah-vehk] (with).

⏸

Solve the math problems below to come up with the answers in French.

1. **deux + neuf =** _____

2. **sept - trois =** _____

3. **soixante et onze + deux =** _____

4. **vingt × deux =** _____

5. (vingt et un × deux) + quinze = _____

6. cinquante + cinquante = _____

ANSWER KEY:
1. onze; 2. quatre; 3. soixante-treize; 4. quarante; 5. cinquante-sept; 6. cent

✎ Drive It Home

A. Fill in the blanks with the appropriate form of être (*to be*). Then read each sentence aloud.

1. Vous _____ étudiant. (*You are a student.*)

2. Il _____ étudiant. (*He is a student.*)

3. Elles _____ étudiantes. (*They are students.*)

4. On _____ étudiants. (*We are students.*)

5. Tu _____ étudiant. (*You are a student.*)

6. Nous _____ étudiants. (*We are students.*)

7. Je _____ étudiant. (*I am a student.*)

8. Elle _____ étudiante. (*She is a student.*)

9. Ils _____ étudiants. (*They are students.*)

B. Good job! Now fill in the blanks with the appropriate subject pronoun (je, tu, il, etc.).

1. _____ sommes étudiants. (*We are students.*)

2. _____ est étudiante. (*She is a student.*)

3. _____ êtes étudiant. (*You are a student.*)

4. _____ sont étudiantes. (*They [feminine] are students.*)

5. _____ es étudiant. (*You are a student.*)

6. _____ suis étudiant. (*I am a student.*)

7. _____ est étudiants. (*We are students.*)

8. _____ est étudiant. (*He is a student.*)

9. _____ sont étudiants. (*They [masculine] are students.*)

ANSWER KEY:
A: 1. êtes; 2. est; 3. sont; 4. est; 5. es; 6. sommes; 7. suis; 8. est; 9. sont
B: 1. Nous; 2. Elle; 3. Vous; 4. Elles; 5. Tu; 6. Je; 7. On; 8. Il; 9. Ils

Parting Words

Congratulations!

Félicitations !

fay-lee-see-tah-syoh(n)

You've finished the lesson! How did you do? You should now be able to:

☐ Count from 1 to 22 (Still unsure? Go back to page 47)

☐ Say *the men* and *the women* (Still unsure? Go back to page 49)

☐ Count from 22 to 1,000 (Still unsure? Go back to page 51)

☐ Say *I am, you are,* etc. (Still unsure? Go back to page 53)

☐ Use what you've learned to describe a photograph (Still unsure? Go back to page 58)

Take It Further

▶ 3J Take It Further (CD 1, Track 32)

In case you want to count a bit higher:

one hundred	cent	sah(n)
two hundred	deux cents	duh sah(n)

three hundred	**trois cents**	trwah sah(n)
one thousand	**mille**	meel
five thousand	**cinq mille**	sa(n) meel
eight thousand	**huit mille**	wee meel

A few other useful numbers are the "ordinals":

premier	pruh-myay	*first*
deuxième*	duh-zyehm	*second*
troisième	trwah-zyehm	*third*
quatrième	kah-tree-yehm	*fourth*
cinquième	sa(n)-kyehm	*fifth*
sixième	see-zyehm	*sixth*
septième	seh-tyehm	*seventh*
huitième	wee-tyehm	*eighth*
neuvième	nuh-vyehm	*ninth*
dixième	dee-zyehm	*tenth*

* Another common way of saying *second* is **second** [suh-goh(n)]. But **deuxième** means *second* in a series of three or more, while **second** means *second* or *last* in a pair.

And that wraps up Lesson 3! Feel free to go back and review, or go on for more French.

Don't forget to go to *www.livinglanguage.com/languagelab* to access your free online tools for this lesson: flashcards, games, and quizzes.

Word Recall

Now let's review vocabulary and grammar from previous lessons.

A. Fill in the blanks using the following words:

suis	sont	appelle	fille	bonjour
est	parle	fils	mari	voilà

_____ ! Je m' _____

_____ Jennifer Mercier. Je _____

_____ américaine. Je _____

un peu français. Je vous présente mon _____, François Mercier.

Il _____ français. Et _____

_____ mes deux enfants: Sophie, ma _____ ,

et Vincent, mon _____ . Ils _____ étudiants.

Hello! My name is Jennifer Mercier. I am American. I speak a little French. Let me introduce my husband, François Mercier. He is French. And there are my two children: Sophie, my daughter, and Vincent, my son. They are students.

B. Translate the following phrases into French.

1. *ten women* _____

2. *one person* _____

3. *one female child* _____

4. *one male child* _____

5. *three brothers* _____

6. *the family* _____

7. *the families* _____

ANSWER KEY:
A: Bonjour; appelle; suis; parle; mari; est; voilà; fille; fils; sont
B: 1. dix femmes; 2. une personne; 3. une enfant; 4. un enfant; 5. trois frères; 6. la famille; 7. les familles

Lesson 4: At Home

Leçon quatre : à la maison

luh-soh(n) kah-truh: ah lah meh-zoh(n)

In this lesson, you'll learn how to:

1 Name common objects around the home

2 Talk about what you *have*
Say how old you are

3 Use what you've learned to talk about
your house and your family

As usual, let's get started with some vocabulary.

1 Name common objects around the home

Vocabulary Builder 1

Note that **dans** [dah(n)] means *in* or *into*.

▶ 4B Vocabulary Builder 1 (CD 1, Track 34)

I have a house.	**J'ai une maison.***	zheh ewn meh-zoh(n)
My house has six rooms.	**Ma maison a six pièces.**	mah meh-zoh(n) ah see pyehs
There is a sofa in the living room.	**Il y a un canapé dans le salon.**	eel ee yah uh(n) kah-nah-pay dah(n) luh sah-loh(n)
There is also a TV and a computer.	**Il y a aussi une télé** et un ordinateur.**	eel ee yah oh-see ewn tay-lay ay uh(n) nohr-dee-nah-tuhr
There is a table in the dining room.	**Il y a une table dans la salle à manger.**	eel ee yah ewn tah-bluh dah(n) lah sahl ah mah(n)-zhay
There is a bed in the bedroom.	**Il y a un lit dans la chambre (à coucher).**	eel ee yah uh(n) lee dah(n) lah shah(m)-bruh (ah koo-shay)
There is a refrigerator in the kitchen.	**Il y a un réfrigérateur dans la cuisine.**	eel ee yah uh(n) ray-free-zhay-rah-tuhr dah(n) lah kwee-zeen
There is a shower in the bathroom.	**Il y a une douche dans la salle de bains.**	eel ee yah ewn doosh dah(n) lah sahl duh ba(n)

* **Maison** can mean both *house* and *home*.
** **Télé** is short for **télévision** [tay-lay-vee-zyoh(n)]. This is similar to *TV* versus *television* in English.

There are books in the library.	Il y a des livres dans la bibliothèque.	eel ee yah day lee-vruh dah(n) lah bee-blee-yoh-tehk
There is wine in the cellar.	Il y a du vin dans la cave.	eel ee yah dew va(n) dah(n) lah kahv
There are flowers in the garden.	Il y a des fleurs dans le jardin.	eel ee yah day fluhr dah(n) luh zhahr-da(n)
And there is a car in the garage.	Et il y a une voiture dans le garage.	ay eel ee yah ewn vwah-tewr dah(n) luh gah-rahzh

✎ Vocabulary Practice 1

Now let's practice what you've learned. As always, fill in the blanks with the correct French translations.

You'll have to do a bit of deciphering on your own for this exercise, but you should see patterns in the list that will help you.

a house, a home _____

a shower _____

a sofa _____

a car _____

a TV _____

the living room _____

a computer _____

the dining room _____

a table _____

the bedroom _____

a bed _____

the kitchen _____

a refrigerator _____

the bathroom _____

the library _____   *the garden* _____

the cellar _____   *the garage* _____

ANSWER KEY:
une maison (*a house, a home*); un canapé (*a sofa*); une télé[vision] (*a TV*); un ordinateur (*a computer*); une table (*a table*); un lit (*a bed*); un réfrigérateur (*a refrigerator*); une douche (*a shower*); une voiture (*a car*); le salon (*the living room*); la salle à manger (*the dining room*); la chambre à coucher (*the bedroom*); la cuisine (*the kitchen*); la salle de bains (*the bathroom*); la bibliothèque (*the library*); la cave (*the cellar*); le jardin (*the garden*); le garage (*the garage*)

Grammar Builder 1
▶ 4C Grammar Builder 1 (CD 1, Track 35)

Let's pause. You just learned a lot of useful vocabulary for talking about the home.

Did you notice *a room* can be called **une pièce** [ewn pyehs], or **une salle** [ewn sahl]? Also note that **bibliothèque** [bee-blee-yoh-tehk] means *library*. The word **librairie** [lee- breh-ree] exists in French, but it means *bookstore*. (Note that **librairie** is a feminine noun.)

Can you remember how to say *in*? You saw it in several sentences. It's **dans** [dah(n)]. With cities, *in* is **à** [ah]:

| à Paris | ah pah-ree | *in Paris* |
| à Montréal | ah moh(n)-ray-ahl | *in Montreal* |

And how about *also*? (Remember it from Lesson 2?) It's **aussi** [oh-see].

Finally, notice that the phrase **il y a** [eel ee yah] (which you were first introduced to in Lesson 3) means *there is* or *there are*.

So, you could say:

| Il y a une belle fleur dans le jardin. | eel ee yah ewn behl fluhr dah(n) luh zhahr-da(n) | *There is a beautiful flower in the garden.* |
| Il y a six pièces dans ma maison aussi. | eel ee yah see pyehs dah(n) mah meh-zoh(n) oh-see | *There are six rooms in my home, too. (There are also six rooms in my home.)* |

A good phrase to know with **il y a** is **beaucoup de**, which means *many* or *a lot of.* You learned it with the plurals (in Lesson 3).

Il y a beaucoup de musées à Paris.
eel ee yah boh-koo duh mew-zay ah pah-ree
There are a lot of museums in Paris.

Take It Further

You also saw the following new words in Vocabulary Builder 1 and Grammar Builder 1:

un musée	uh(n) mew-zay	*a museum*
un livre	uh(n) lee-vruh	*a book*
le vin	luh va(n)	*the wine*
une fleur	ewn fluhr	*a flower*
du	dew	*some, of the (masculine)*
des	day	*some, of the (plural)*

Like **le, la,** and **les, du** and **des** are used more often in French than in English, and they aren't always translated into English. In fact, while the use of a word like *some* is generally optional in English, it is usually required in French:

Il y a du vin dans la cave.

eel ee yah dew va(n) dah(n) lah kahv

There is wine in the cellar./There is some wine in the cellar.

Note that **des** is also used in French as the plural of **un/une**. For example, you would say **une fleur** (*a flower*) and **des fleurs** (*flowers*). There isn't really an equivalent to this in English since a plural of *a/an* doesn't exist. You'll learn more about other uses of **du** and **des** in Lesson 7.

2 Talk about what you *have*
Say how old you are

Vocabulary Builder 2

▶ 4D Vocabulary Builder 2 (CD 1, Track 36)

Jean and Marie have a big apartment.	**Jean et Marie ont un grand* appartement.**	zhah(n) ay mah-ree oh(n) tuh(n) grah(n) tah-pahr-tuh-mah(n)
The living room has a (grandfather) clock.	**Le salon a une pendule.**	luh sah-loh(n) ah ewn pah(n)-dewl
The library has a computer.	**La bibliothèque a un ordinateur.**	lah bee-blee-yoh-tehk ah uh(n) nohr-dee-nah-tuhr
The bathroom has a mirror.	**La salle de bains a un miroir.**	lah sahl duh ba(n) ah uh(n) mee-rwahr
The kitchen has a microwave (oven).	**La cuisine a un micro-ondes.**	lah kwee-zeen ah uh(n) mee-kroh-oh(n)d

* **Grand** [grah(n)] can mean *big* or *tall*. Like **petit** and **petite**, **grand** also has another form: **grande** [grah(n)d]. Again, you'll learn more in Lesson 5.

✎ Vocabulary Practice 2

Fill in the blanks with the correct French translations. Again, you may have to do a bit of deciphering on your own, but you should see patterns in the list that will help you.

an apartment _____   *a mirror* _____

a (grandfather) clock _____   *a microwave (oven)* _____

ANSWER KEY:
un appartement (*an apartment*); une pendule (*a grandfather clock*); un miroir (*a mirror*); un micro-ondes (*a microwave*)

Grammar Builder 2

▶ 4E Grammar Builder 2 (CD 1, Track 37)

Now let's take a closer look at the forms of avoir [ah-vwahr], *to have.*

AVOIR *(TO HAVE)*		
I have	j'ai	zheh
you have (familiar)	tu as	tew ah
he has, she has	il a, elle a	eel ah, ehl ah
we have	nous avons	noo zah-voh(n)
you have (polite/plural)	vous avez	voo zah-vay
they have (masculine, feminine)	ils ont, elles ont	eel zoh(n), ehl zoh(n)

Notice that in French you use avoir to give an age:

J'ai trente ans.

zheh trah(n)t ah(n)

I'm thirty years old. (literally, I have thirty years.)

It's also used in many other common expressions where English uses a form
of *to be*:

j'ai chaud	zheh shoh	*I'm hot*
j'ai froid	zheh frwah	*I'm cold*
j'ai sommeil	zheh soh-mehy	*I'm sleepy*
j'ai peur	zheh puhr	*I'm afraid*
j'ai raison	zheh reh-zoh(n)	*I'm right*
j'ai tort	zheh tohr	*I'm wrong*

Take It Further

Remember that **on** uses the same form as **il** and **elle**. So for **avoir**, you would say
on a (*we have, people in general have, one has*).

And remember that **il/elle** can also mean *it (masculine/feminine)*, so **il a/elle a** can
mean *it has*.

✎ Work Out 1

Okay, let's put everything you've learned so far together in a short comprehension
exercise. Form sentences by matching up the phrases that ***best*** go together.

▶ 4F Work Out 1 (CD 1, Track 38). Listen to the audio to practice pronouncing these and
other phrases. The audio includes the completed sentences, so try to do the exercise
here first before listening.

1. Il y a beaucoup de vin...   a. ... dans la chambre (à coucher).

2. Il y a une douche...   b. ... dans la cave.

3. Ils ont un canapé...   c. ... dans la salle de bains.

4. Elle a un grand lit...   d. ... dans le salon.

ANSWER KEY:

1. b (**Il y a beaucoup de vin dans la cave.** *There is a lot of wine in the cellar.*) 2. c (**Il y a une douche dans la salle de bains.** *There is a shower in the bathroom.*) 3. d (**Ils ont un canapé dans le salon.** *They have a sofa in the living room.*); 4. a (**Elle a un grand lit dans la chambre à coucher.** *She has a big bed in the bedroom.*)

3 Use what you've learned to talk about your house and your family

Bring It All Together

Now let's bring it all together and add a little bit more vocabulary and structure. Read and listen to the following monologue about Antoine's house and family.

▶ 4G Bring It All Together (CD 1, Track 39)

Hi! My name is Antoine.
Salut ! Je m'appelle Antoine.
sah-lew! zhuh mah-pehl ah(n)-twahn

I have a big family.
J'ai une grande famille.
zheh ewn grah(n)d fah-meey

And we have a big house.
Et nous avons une grande maison.
ay noo zah-voh(n) ewn grah(n)d meh-zoh(n)

My father has a new car.
Mon père a une nouvelle voiture.
moh(n) pehr ah ewn noo-vehl vwah-tewr

And my mother has a new computer.

Et ma mère a un nouvel ordinateur.

ay mah mehr ah uh(n) noo-vehl ohr-dee-nah-tuhr

My brother is thirteen years old.

Mon frère a treize ans.

moh(n) frehr ah trehz ah(n)

He has a lot of friends.

Il a beaucoup d'amis.

eel ah boh-koo dah-mee

My sister is eight.

Ma sœur a huit ans.

mah suhr ah wee tah(n)

She has a lot of video games.

Elle a beaucoup de jeux vidéo.

ehl ah boh-koo duh zhuh vee-day-oh

And me, I have a little dog.

Et moi, j'ai un petit chien.

ay mwah, zheh uh(n) puh-tee shya(n)

Take It Further

Let's look at a few new words from Bring It All Together before we practice what you've learned:

nouveau/nouvel/ nouvelle	noo-voh/noo-vehl/noo- vehl	*new*

un jeu	uh(n) zhuh	*a game*
un jeu vidéo	uh(n) zhuh vee-day-oh	*a video game*
un chien	uh(n) shya(n)	*a dog*

You also saw **moi** [mwah] (*me*) again, which you first saw in Lesson 2.

✎ Work Out 2

▶ 4H Work Out 2 (CD 1, Track 40) for different, audio-only exercises!

Let's practice identifying the rooms of a house. Fill in the floor plan below with the correct French word for each room.

1. _____

2. _____

3. _____

4. _____

ANSWER KEY:
1. la chambre (à coucher) (*the bedroom*); 2 la salle de bains (*the bathroom*); 3. le salon (*the living room*); 4. la cuisine (*the kitchen*)

✎ Drive It Home

Fill in the blanks with the appropriate forms of **avoir** (*to have*) and don't forget to read each sentence aloud once you're done.

1. Ils _____ quinze ans. (*They're fifteen years old.*)

2. On _____ quinze ans. (*We are fifteen years old.*)

3. Vous _____ quinze ans. (*You are fifteen years old.*)

4. Elle _____ quinze ans. (*She is fifteen years old.*)

5. J' _____ quinze ans. (*I am fifteen years old.*)

6. Il _____ quinze ans. (*He is fifteen years old.*)

7. Tu _____ quinze ans. (*You are fifteen years old.*)

8. Nous _____ quinze ans. (*We are fifteen years old.*)

9. Elles _____ quinze ans. (*They are fifteen years old.*)

ANSWER KEY:
1. ont; 2. a; 3. avez; 4. a; 5. ai; 6. a; 7. as; 8. avons; 9. ont

Parting Words

▶ 41 Parting Words (CD 1, Track 41)

You've finished the lesson! How did you do? You should now be able to:

☐ Name common objects around the home (Still unsure? Go back to page 66)

☐ Talk about what you *have* (Still unsure? Go back to page 71)

☐ Say how old you are (Still unsure? Go back to page 71)

☐ Use what you've learned to talk about your house and your family
(Still unsure? Go back to page 73)

Now you know plenty of **vocabulaire** [voh-kah-bew-lehr]—that means **beaucoup de mots** [boh-koo duh moh] (*a lot of words*). And you can put them together in sentences, because you know **beaucoup de grammaire aussi** [boh-koo duh grah-mehr oh-see].

You're already speaking French!

If you're ready for Lesson 5, go right ahead. If you'd like to review, you can do that, too!

Ⅱ

🖱 Don't forget to go to *www.livinglanguage.com/languagelab* to access your free online tools for this lesson: flashcards, games, and quizzes.

Word Recall

Now let's review vocabulary and expressions from previous lessons. Choose the correct English translation for each of the following French expressions.

1. **Ça va mal.**

   a. *It's going well.*
   b. *It's not going well.*
   c. *I'm fine.*
   d. *Not bad.*

2. **J'ai peur.**

   a. *I'm cold.*
   b. *I'm wrong.*
   c. *I'm afraid.*
   d. *I'm hot.*

3. **Comment allez-vous ?**

   a. *How are you? (polite)*
   b. *What's your name? (polite)*
   c. *How are you? (familiar)*
   d. *What's your name? (familiar)*

4. **Il y a quarante livres.**

   a. *He has fourteen books.*
   b. *He has forty books.*
   c. *There are fourteen books.*
   d. *There are forty books.*

5. **Elle est étudiante.**

   a. *They are students.*
   b. *She is a student.*
   c. *We are students.*
   d. *He is a student.*

6. **Je ne comprends pas...**

   a. *My name is ...*
   b. *I don't speak ...*
   c. *I don't understand ...*
   d. *It's going well ...*

ANSWER KEY:
1. b; 2. c; 3. a; 4. d; 5. b; 6. c

Lesson 5: Describing Things

Leçon cinq : les descriptions

luh-soh(n) sa(n)k: lay deh-skreep-syoh(n)

In this lesson, you'll learn how to:

1 Describe something or someone

2 Describe more than one person or thing
Say *my*, *your*, *his*, *her*, etc.

3 Use what you've learned to describe **la Joconde**
[lah zhoh-koh(n)d] (*the Mona Lisa*)

First, let's get started with a few simple descriptive adjectives.

1 Describe something or someone

Vocabulary Builder 1

You'll see two forms of each French adjective: masculine and feminine. We'll come back to how to use them in a moment. Ready?

▶ 5B Vocabulary Builder 1 (CD 1, Track 43)

*big**	**grand/grande**	grah(n)/grah(n)d
*small**	**petit/petite**	puh-tee/puh-teet
good	**bon/bonne**	boh(n)/bohn
bad	**mauvais/mauvaise**	moh-veh/moh-vehz
red	**rouge/rouge**	roozh/roozh
white	**blanc/blanche**	blah(n)/blah(n)sh
blue	**bleu/bleue**	bluh/bluh
new	**nouveau/nouvelle**	noo-voh/noo-vehl
old	**vieux/vieille**	vyuh/vyehy
handsome, beautiful	**beau/belle**	boh/behl
American	**américain/américaine**	ah-may-ree-ka(n)/ ah-may-ree-kehn
French	**français/française**	frah(n)-seh/frah(n)-sehz

* As you know, **grand/grande** can mean both big and tall, and **petit/petite** can mean *small, little,* or *short.*

✎ Vocabulary Practice 1

Now let's practice the adjectives you just learned. As always, fill in the blanks with the correct French translations.

Make sure to include both forms of each adjective.

big, tall _____

small, short, little _____

good _____

bad _____

red _____

white _____

blue _____

new _____

old _____

handsome, beautiful _____

American _____

French _____

ANSWER KEY:
grand/grande (*big, tall*); petit/petite (*small, short, little*); bon/bonne (*good*); mauvais/mauvaise (*bad*); rouge/rouge (*red*); blanc/blanche (*white*); bleu/bleue (*blue*); nouveau/nouvelle (*new*); vieux/vieille (*old*); beau/belle (*handsome, beautiful*); américain/américaine (*American*); français/française (*French*)

Grammar Builder 1
5C Grammar Builder 1 (CD 1, Track 44)

Okay, let's stop there.

Adjectives in French have to agree with the noun they describe. That means that you have to use a masculine singular adjective with a masculine singular noun, as in:

MASCULINE SINGULAR		
un homme français	uh(n) nohm frah(n)-seh	*a French man*

And a feminine singular adjective with a feminine singular noun, as in:

FEMININE SINGULAR		
une femme française	ewn fahm frah(n)-sehz	*a French woman*

You usually add an -e to the masculine to get the feminine (français + -e = française).

In pronunciation, that usually means that a consonant ending that's silent in the masculine, like the -s in français [frah(n)-seh] or the -d in grand [grah(n)], will be pronounced in the feminine:

française	frah-sehz
grande	grah(n)d

If an adjective already ends in -e in the masculine singular, like rouge (or suisse, remember?), the feminine is the same.

In some cases, you double the final consonant and add an -e (bon/bonne), and in other cases there are irregulars, like:

vieux/vieille	old
blanc/blanche	white
nouveau/nouvelle	new

Take It Further

Beau (*beautiful, handsome*) is obviously another example of an adjective with an irregular form in the feminine: belle. You may have also noticed that a third form of *beautiful* was introduced in Lesson 3: bel [behl]. Furthermore, you saw *new* written as nouvel [noo-vehl] in Lesson 4.

Nouvel and bel are special forms of the adjective. They're used with masculine nouns that begin with a vowel or silent h (see the Pronunciation Guide for more information on the "silent h").

un nouvel ami	a new friend
un bel homme	a handsome man

Same goes for *old*, which uses vieil [vyehy] with those types of masculine nouns.

Apart from *beautiful, new,* and *old*, most adjectives don't have special forms for nouns like that. They just use their regular masculine singular forms.

2 Describe more than one person or thing
Say *my, your, his, her,* etc.

Vocabulary Builder 2
▶ 5D Vocabulary Builder 2 (CD 2, Track 1)

an athletic boy	**un garçon sportif**	uh(n) gahr-soh(n) spohr-teef
an athletic girl	**une fille sportive**	ewn feey spohr-teev
a happy boy	**un garçon heureux**	uh(n) gahr-soh(n) uh-ruh
a happy girl	**une fille heureuse**	ewn feey uh-ruhz
my old grandfather	**mon vieux grand-père**	moh(n) vyuh grah(n)-pehr
my dear mother	**ma chère* mère**	mah shehr mehr
my charming children	**mes charmants enfants**	may shahr-mah(n) zah(n)-fah(n)
an amusing game	**un jeu amusant**	uh(n) zhuh ah-mew-zah(n)
a beautiful house	**une belle maison**	ewn behl meh-zoh(n)
a red car	**une voiture rouge**	ewn vwah-tewr roozh
a new sofa	**un nouveau canapé**	uh(n) noo-voh kah-nah-pay
a good library	**une bonne bibliothèque**	ewn bohn bee-blee-yoh-tehk

⬛ * The masculine form of chère is cher. Cher/chère can also mean *expensive.*

✎ Vocabulary Practice 2

Fill in the blanks with the correct French translations. Try to include **both** the masculine and feminine forms of each adjective.

(Hint: the masculine singular forms of *amusing* and *charming* are amusant and charmant. Those adjectives form the feminine singular normally, so you should be able to fill in the feminine forms based on what you learned in Grammar Builder 1.)

athletic _____   charming _____

happy _____   amusing _____

dear, expensive _____

ANSWER KEY:
sportif/sportive (*athletic*); heureux/heureuse (*happy*); cher/chère (*dear, expensive*); charmant/charmante (*charming*); amusant/amusante (*amusing*)

Grammar Builder 2
5E Grammar Builder 2 (CD 2, Track 2)

You probably noticed that most French adjectives come *after* the noun they describe, but a few common ones come *before* it, like:*

grand/grande	grah(n)/grah(n)d	*big*
petit/petite	puh-tee/puh-teet	*small*
bon/bonne	boh(n)/bohn	*good*
mauvais/mauvaise	moh-veh/moh-vehz	*bad*
beau/belle	boh/behl	*beautiful*
vieux/vieille	vyuh/vyehy	*old*
nouveau/nouvelle	noo-voh/noo-vehl	*new*

* Note that the adjective charmant/charmante [shahr-mah(n)/shahr-mah(n)t] (*charming*) can come before *or* after a noun. You'll learn more if you bought *Complete French* and are continuing on to *Intermediate French*.

Adjectives also have to agree in number (with the noun), but the good news is, the pronunciation is just about always the same in the plural as it is in the singular. In writing, there's usually an -s added. So:

MASCULINE		
le garçon sportif	luh gahr-soh(n) spohr-teef	*the athletic boy*
les garçons sportifs	lay gahr-soh(n) spohr-teef	*the athletic boys*

In the feminine, we have:

FEMININE		
la fille sportive	lah feey spohr-teev	*the athletic girl*
les filles sportives	lay feey spohr-teev	*the athletic girls*

(Note that French adjectives—and nouns!—that already end in -s in the masculine singular, don't change in the masculine plural: le garçon français and les garçons français.)

You probably also noticed the possessive mon/ma (*my*). Now let's look at some other possessives, which agree in gender and number with the **possession** (not the person who's speaking or who has the item).

mon/ma	moh(n)/mah	*my*
ton/ta	toh(n)/tah	*your (familiar)*
son/sa	soh(n)/sah	*his, her,* or *its*

For plural possessions (*my cars* instead of *my car*), use:

mes	may	*my*
tes	tay	*your (familiar)*
ses	say	*his, her,* or *its*

Let's see some examples:

my father and my mother	mon père et ma mère	moh(n) pehr ay mah mehr
your brother and your sister	ton frère et ta sœur	toh(n) frehr ay tah suhr
his/her bike	son vélo	soh(n) vay-loh
his/her car	sa voiture	sah vwah-tewr
my notebooks	mes cahiers	may kah-yay
your friends	tes amis	tay zah-mee
his/her things	ses choses	say shohz

(Note that mes, tes, and ses can be used with both masculine plural nouns—such as cahiers and amis—and feminine plural nouns—such as choses.)

Did you notice the pronunciation of tes amis? The -s (in tes) is usually silent: tes [tay]. But if the next word begins with a vowel sound, that -s is pronounced: tes amis [tay zah-mee]. This happens a lot in French, and not just with -s:

mes amis	may zah-mee	my friends
ses amis	say zah-mee	his/her friends
mon ami	moh(n) nah-mee	my friend
ton ami	toh(n) nah-mee	your friend

And so on.

(Don't forget to listen to the audio for a clearer understanding of this pronunciation! Also check out the Pronunciation Guide at the end of the book for more information on why the -s and -n sounds are pronounced with the following word.)

Finally, we have:

notre	noh-truh	*our*
votre	voh-truh	*your (plural/polite)*
leur	luhr	*their*

These forms are used for both masculine and feminine singular possessions:

notre maison	noh-truh meh-zoh(n)	*our house*
votre voiture	voh-truh vwah-tewr	*your car*
leur ami	luhr ah-mee	*their friend*

For plural possessions, use:

nos	noh	*our*
vos	voh	*your (plural/polite)*
leurs	luhr	*their*

Here are some examples:

our father and our mother	**notre père et notre mère**	noh-truh pehr ay noh-truh mehr
our parents	**nos parents**	noh pah-rah(n)
your brother and your sister	**votre frère et votre sœur**	voh-truh frehr ay voh-truh suhr
your friends	**vos amis**	voh zah-mee
their car and their bike	**leur voiture et leur vélo**	luhr vwah-tewr ay luhr vay-loh
their things	**leurs choses**	luhr shohz

It is also important to mention that **mon** (*my*), **ton** (*your*), and **son** (*his/her*) are not just used with masculine singular nouns. They are also used with feminine singular nouns that begin with a vowel or silent **h** (don't forget to go to the

Pronunciation Guide at the end of the book for more information on the "silent h"). For example:

| *my female friend* | **mon amie** | moh(n) nah-mee |

You would not say ma amie.

And note that you can also talk about possessions by using the word de [duh] (*of, from, for*):

C'est le frère de Marie.
seh luh frehr duh mah-ree
This is Marie's brother. (literally, This is the brother of Marie.)

Voilà le livre de Paul.
vwah-lah luh lee-vruh duh pohl
Here is Paul's book.

Take It Further

So, just to clarify, because this is important, French possessive adjectives agree with the **possession**. For example, a French possessive adjective would agree with the word *car* in *his car*, and **not** with the person who is speaking or who owns the car. So you would use the feminine sa in sa voiture (*his/her car*) because voiture (*car*) is a feminine noun; it doesn't matter whether a man or a woman owns the car. This is different from English, where the possessive sometimes depends on who has the possession: *his car* or *her car*.

And you would use ses if there is more than one car: ses voitures (*his/her cars*). Ses is used with both masculine and feminine nouns. Again, this is different from English, where the possessive adjective doesn't change between singular and plural: *his car, his cars*.

Now let's quickly review some of the new words you saw in Grammar Builder 2:

un vélo	uh(n) vay-loh	a bike
un cahier	uh(n) kah-yay	a notebook
une chose	ewn shohz	a thing
un parent	uh(n) pah-rah(n)	a parent, a relative

✎ Work Out 1

Translate the following sentences using the words that you've learned plus the new words from the word bank below:

nice, kind	gentil/gentille	zhah(n)-tee/zhah(n)-teey
generous	généreux/généreuse	zhay-nay-ruh/ zhay-nay-ruhz
Canadian	canadien/canadienne	kah-nah-dya(n)/ kah-nah-dyehn
a company, a firm	une firme	ewn feerm
a boss	un patron/une patronne	uh(n) pah-troh(n)/ ewn pah-trohn
a colleague	un collègue/une collègue	uh(n) koh-lehg/ ewn koh-lehg
a flag	un drapeau	uh(n) drah-poh

▶ 5F Work Out 1 (CD 2, Track 3). Listen to the audio to practice pronouncing the sentences below! Of course, the audio also includes the French translations, so try to complete the exercise here first before listening.

1. *I am French. (masculine)* _____

2. *I am French. (feminine)* _____

3. *My flag is blue, white, and red.* _____

_____

4. *You are American. (familiar, feminine)* _____

5. *Your flag is red, white, and blue. (familiar)* _____

_____

6. *He is Canadian.* _____

7. *His flag is white and red.* _____

8. *My company is good and generous.* _____

_____

9. *My (male) boss is nice.* _____

10. *My (male) colleagues are athletic.* _____

ANSWER KEY:
1. **Je suis français.** 2. **Je suis française.** 3. **Mon drapeau est bleu, blanc et rouge.** 4. **Tu es américaine.**
5. **Ton drapeau est rouge, blanc et bleu.** 6. **Il est canadien.** 7. **Son drapeau est blanc et rouge.**
8. **Ma firme est bonne et généreuse.** 9. **Mon patron est gentil.** 10. **Mes collègues sont sportifs.**

3 Use what you've learned to describe **la Joconde** [lah zhoh-koh(n)d] (*the Mona Lisa*)

Bring It All Together

Now let's bring it all together and add a little bit more vocabulary and structure.
Read and listen to the following dialogue between two friends looking at the
Mona Lisa.

▶ 5G Bring It All Together (CD 2, Track 4)

A: *I'm admiring an old painting.*
J'admire un vieux tableau.
zhah-dmeer uh(n) vyuh tah-bloh

B: *It's the Mona Lisa.*
C'est la Joconde.
seh lah zhoh-koh(n)d

A: *She is beautiful.*
Elle est belle.
ehl eh behl

B: *Her smile is mysterious.*
Son sourire est mystérieux.
soh(n) soo-reer eh mee-stay-ryuh

A: *Her hair is black.*
Ses cheveux sont noirs.
say shuh-vuh soh(n) nwahr

B: *Her skin is very white.*
Sa peau est très blanche.
sah poh eh treh blah(n)sh

A: *What are your favorite paintings?*
Quels sont tes tableaux préférés ?
kehl soh(n) tay tah-bloh pray-fay-ray

B: *Paintings are expensive.*
Les tableaux sont chers.
lay tah-bloh soh(n) shehr

Take It Further

Let's look at some of the new words you saw in Bring It All Together, starting with:

quel/quelle (*singular*), quels/quelles (*plural*)	kehl	*what, which*

You'll learn more about quel and its different forms in the next lesson. And did you remember très [treh] from Lesson 1? It means *very*.

Here are some other new words that you saw:

J'admire...	zhahd-meer	*I admire .../ I'm admiring ...*
un tableau	uh(n) tah-bloh	*a painting*
un sourire	uh(n) soo-reer	*a smile*
mystérieux/ mystérieuse	mee-stay-ryuh/ mee-stay-ryuhz	*mysterious*
préféré/préférée	pray-fay-ray/pray-fay-ray	*favorite*
noir/noire	nwahr/nwahr	*black*
un cheveu	uh(n) shuh-vuh	*a hair (single strand)*
les cheveux	lay shuh-vuh	*hair*
la peau	lah poh	*the skin*

Unlike most French nouns, the plural of tableau ends in -x, not -s. Similarly, the plural of cheveu is cheveux. Many words that end in -eau and -eu, and some words that end in -ou, add -x in the plural instead of -s.

For example:

SINGULAR		PLURAL	
le gâteau luh gah-toh	the cake	les gâteaux lay gah-toh	the cakes
le jeu luh zhuh	the game	les jeux lay zhuh	the games
le bijou luh bee-zhoo	the jewel	les bijoux lay bee-zhoo	the jewels, the jewelry

The good news is that, like the -s plural ending, the -x plural ending is normally silent when speaking.

Work Out 2

5H Work Out 2 (CD 2, Track 5) for different, audio-only exercises! Do the exercise here first before doing the audio exercises.

Match the English adjectives to their correct French translations:

1. *nice*	a. **grand**
2. *red*	b. **heureux**
3. *big*	c. **riche**
4. *happy*	d. **gentil**
5. *small*	e. **bon**
6. *good*	f. **intelligent**
7. *intelligent*	g. **rouge**
8. *rich*	h. **petit**

Okay, you hadn't been introduced to **riche** [reesh] or **intelligent** [a(n)-teh-lee-zhah(n)] yet, but they were pretty easy to figure out, weren't they? Fortunately,

French has many words that are very similar to English, like la table, le restaurant, l'animal, l'université, etc. So you already know a lot of French vocabulary just by knowing English! Just be careful though; there are "false" similar words too, like la librairie (*the bookstore*) and le collège (*the secondary school, the junior high school, the middle school*).

ANSWER KEY:
1. d; 2. g; 3. a; 4. b; 5. h; 6. e; 7. f; 8. c

✎ Drive It Home

A. Rewrite the following French sentences by putting the adjectives in the feminine. Don't forget to read each sentence aloud once you're done. Ready?

1. Je suis français. (*I am French.*) _____

2. Je suis américain. (*I am American.*) _____

3. Je suis grand. (*I am big.*) _____

4. Je suis petit. (*I am small.*) _____

5. Je suis mauvais. (*I am bad.*) _____

6. Je suis amusant. (*I am amusing.*) _____

7. Je suis beau. (*I am handsome.*) _____

8. Je suis vieux. (*I am old.*) _____

B. Now fill in the blanks with either mon, ma, or mes.

1. _____ cuisine est nouvelle. (*My kitchen is new.*)

2. _____ amie est heureuse. (*My friend is happy.*)

3. _____ frère est intelligent. (*My brother is intelligent.*)

4. _____ parents sont gentils. (*My parents/relatives are nice.*)

5. _____ drapeau est bleu, blanc et rouge. (*My flag is blue, white, and red.*)

6. _____ tableaux sont chers. (*My paintings are expensive.*)

7. _____ voiture est noire. (*My car is black.*)

8. _____ femme est charmante. (*My wife is charming.*)

ANSWER KEY:
A. 1. Je suis française. 2. Je suis américaine. 3. Je suis grande. 4. Je suis petite. 5. Je suis mauvaise.
6. Je suis amusante. 7. Je suis belle. 8. Je suis vieille.
B. 1. Ma; 2. Mon; 3. Mon; 4. Mes; 5. Mon; 6. Mes; 7. Ma; 8. Ma

Parting Words

Congratulations!

Félicitations !

fay-lee-see-tah-syoh(n)

You've finished the lesson! You've learned the basic vocabulary and grammar you need to describe things.

How did you do? You should now be able to:

☐ Describe something or someone (Still unsure? Go back to page 82)

☐ Describe more than one person or thing (Still unsure? Go back to page 86)

☐ Say *my, your, his, her*, etc. (Still unsure? Go back to page 86)

☐ Use what you've learned to describe la Joconde (Don't know what la Joconde is? Go back to page 91)

Take It Further

▶ 5J Take It Further (CD 2, Track 7)

Here are some other descriptive terms you can use, in both their masculine and feminine forms:

chaud/chaude	shoh/shohd	hot
froid/froide	frwah/frwahd	cold
laid/laide	leh/lehd	ugly
long/longue	loh(n)/loh(n)g	long
court/courte	koor/koort	short
fort/forte	fohr/fohrt	strong
doux/douce	doo/doos	sweet, soft
haut/haute	oh/oht	high
bas/basse	bah/bahs	low
délicieux/délicieuse	day-lee-syuh/ day-lee-syuhz	delicious

A few others have the same forms for both genders:

facile	fah-seel	easy
difficile	dee-fee-seel	difficult
malade	mah-lahd	sick
jeune	zhuhn	young
triste	treest	sad
pauvre	poh-vruh	poor
sale	sahl	dirty
propre	proh-pruh	clean

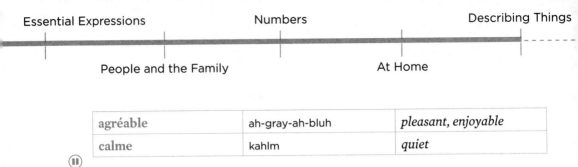

| agréable | ah-gray-ah-bluh | *pleasant, enjoyable* |
| calme | kahlm | *quiet* |

Don't forget to go to *www.livinglanguage.com/languagelab* to access your free online tools for this lesson: flashcards, games, and quizzes.

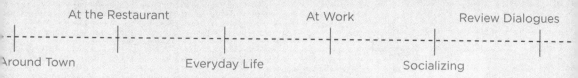
Word Recall

For this Word Recall, let's focus on grammar and review one of the most important verbs in French.

Fill in the following table with all of the forms of **avoir** (*to have*):

I have	
you have (familiar)	
he has, it has (masculine)	
she has, it has (feminine)	
we have, one has, people in general have	
we have	
you have (polite/plural)	
they have (masculine)	
they have (feminine)	

ANSWER KEY:

j'ai; tu as; il a; elle a; on a; nous avons; vous avez; ils ont; elles ont

Quiz 1

Petit Test 1
puh-tee tehst uh(n)

You've made it halfway through the course! Congratulations!

Now let's see how you've done so far. In this section you'll find a short quiz testing what you learned in Lessons 1-5. After you've answered all of the questions, score your quiz and see how you did! If you find that you need to go back and review, please do so before continuing on to Lesson 6.

You'll get a second quiz after Lesson 10, followed by a final review with five dialogues and comprehension questions.

Let's get started!

A. Match the following English words to the correct French translations:

1. la maison	a. *the kitchen*
2. la chambre (à coucher)	b. *the house/home*
3. la salle de bains	c. *the room*
4. la cuisine	d. *the bedroom*
5. la pièce	e. *the bathroom*

B. Translate the following English expressions into French.

1. *What is your name? (polite)*

   _____

2. *Pleased to meet you. (said by a woman)*

   _____

3. *How's it going?*

   _____

4. *Repeat (that), please. (polite)*

   _____

5. *I am twenty-two years old.*

   _____

C. Fill in the blanks with le, la, les, or l':

1. _____ personne

2. _____ garçon

3. _____ enfant

4. _____ sœurs

5. _____ homme

D. Fill in the table with the correct forms of être (*to be*):

I am	1.
you are (familiar)	2.
she is, it is (feminine)	3.
you are (polite/plural)	4.
they are (masculine)	5.

How Did You Do?

Give yourself a point for every correct answer, then use the following key to determine whether or not you're ready to move on:

0-7 points: It's probably best to go back and study the lessons again to make sure you understood everything completely. Take your time; it's not a race! Make sure you spend time reviewing the vocabulary and reading through each Grammar Builder section carefully.

8-16 points: If the questions you missed were in sections A or B, you may want to review the vocabulary from previous lessons; if you missed answers mostly in sections C or D, check the Grammar Builder sections to make sure you have your grammar basics down.

17-20 points: Feel free to move on to Lesson 6! You're doing a great job.

	Points

Lesson 6: Around Town

Leçon six : en ville

In this lesson, you'll learn how to:

1 Ask questions

2 Ask for directions
Understand directions

3 Use what you've learned to get around Paris

Let's get started with some basic question words. Ready? **On y va !** (*Let's go!*)

1 Ask questions

Vocabulary Builder 1

Remember that, from this point on, there won't be any more phonetics. However, just continue listening to the audio to learn and practice pronunciation and you'll do great! Don't be afraid to listen to each track as many times as you need to.

▶ 6B Vocabulary Builder 1 (CD 2, Track 9)

Where?	**Où ?**
Where is the Eiffel Tower, please?	**Où est la Tour Eiffel, s'il vous plaît ?**
Where is Sacré Cœur?	**Où se trouve le Sacré-Cœur ?**
Which? (What?)	**Quel/Quelle ?**
Which is the subway station for the Arc de Triomphe?	**Quelle est la station de métro pour l'Arc de Triomphe ?**
Which is the bus stop for the Louvre museum?	**Quel est l'arrêt de bus pour le musée du Louvre ?**
How?	**Comment ?**
How does one get to the post office? (literally, How does one go to the post office?)	**Comment va-t-on à la poste ?***
Who?	**Qui ?**
Who is the guide?	**Qui est le guide ?**
What... ?	**Qu'est-ce que... ?**
What do you want to do?	**Qu'est-ce que vous voulez faire ?**

* Remember that the pronoun **on** means *one, people in general,* and *we.* To review pronouns, see Lesson 3.

✎ Vocabulary Practice 1

Let's practice! As always, fill in the blanks with the correct French translations.

Don't forget to put a space in between the French word and the quotation mark. If a word has two forms, make sure to include both of them.

Where? _____   *How?* _____

Which?/What? _____   *Who?* _____

_____   *What?* _____

ANSWER KEY:
Où ? (*Where?*); Quel/Quelle ? (*Which?/What?*); Comment ? (*How?*); Qui ? (*Who?*); Qu'est-ce que...? (*What?*)

Grammar Builder 1

▶ 6C Grammar Builder 1 (CD 2, Track 10)

Okay, you've just learned a few useful question words:

où	*where*
quel/quelle	*which (what)*
comment	*how*
qui	*who*
qu'est-ce que	*what*

Notice that you can ask *where* things are in two ways:

1. *By using the verb* être, *as in:*

   où est... ?
   where is ... ?

où sont... ?
where are ... ?

2. *Or you can say* où se trouve... ? *which asks specifically where something is located.*

To ask *what*, start a sentence with qu'est-ce que... A useful question to know is qu'est-ce que c'est ? (*what is this?*)

The question word quel (*which*) is like the adjectives that you've learned; it actually agrees with the noun it's asking about (quel homme–*which man*, quelle maison–*which house*).

Finally, since we're talking about questions, let's go over asking "yes-no questions."

We'll use the sentence vous êtes de Paris (*you're from Paris*) as a starting point. You can ask *are you from Paris?* in three different ways.

1. *Switch the order of the subject (such as* vous*) and verb (such as* êtes*):*

Êtes-vous de Paris ?
Are you from Paris?

(This is often called "inversion.")

2. *Begin the question with* Est-ce que... ? (*no direct translation*)

Est-ce que vous êtes de Paris ?
Are you from Paris?

3. *Simply use question intonation.*

Vous êtes de Paris ?
Are you from Paris? (literally, You are from Paris?)

To answer *yes*, say:

Oui, je suis de Paris.
Yes, I'm from Paris.

To answer *no*, put **ne** (or **n'** before a vowel or silent **h**) and **pas** around the verb:

Non, je ne suis pas de Paris.
No, I'm not from Paris.

⏸

Take It Further

If you use "inversion" to ask a question, then there is an additional rule you should know about. If the verb ends with a vowel, and the pronoun is **il**, **elle**, or **on**, then **-t-** needs to be inserted in between the verb and the pronoun:

Elle a le livre. A-t-elle le livre ?
She has the book. Does she have the book?

Comment va-t-on à la poste ?
How does one get to the post office?

Notice in that last example that the question word **comment** (*how*) is followed by inversion. Many question words are often followed by **est-ce que**, inversion, or sometimes just a verb, as you've seen.

Also, although **qu'est-ce que... ?** does mean *what?*, it's important to mention that it can't be used on its own. It must be followed by something: **Qu'est-ce que vous voulez faire ?** (*What do you want to do?*) If you want to simply ask *What?*, you should instead say:

Quoi ?
What?

Note that **vous voulez** (*you want*) is a form of the verb **vouloir** (*to want*). You'll learn more about this useful verb in Lesson 10. **Faire** (*to do, to make*) is another common and important verb. You'll learn about it in Lesson 8.

Finally, remember that **à** means *in*. You were introduced to it in Lesson 4. As you can see, **à** also means *to* or *at*. Also, **pour** means *for* or *to*.

2 Ask for directions
Understand directions

Vocabulary Builder 2
6D Vocabulary Builder 2 (CD 2, Track 11)

Is the post office far from here?	Est-ce que la poste est loin d'ici ?
No, it's not far.	Non, ce n'est pas loin.
It's very close. (It's very near.)	C'est tout près.
Is the train station close to here? (Is the train station near here/nearby?)	Est-ce que la gare est près d'ici ?
No, it's farther.	Non, c'est plus loin.
Is this the Île de la Cité?	Est-ce que c'est l'Île de la Cité ?

No, you have to cross the bridge.	Non, il faut traverser le pont.
Is this the way to Beaubourg? (literally, Is this the direction of Beaubourg?)	Est-ce que c'est la direction de Beaubourg ?
Yes, go straight ahead.	Oui, allez tout droit.
Turn right. (literally, Turn to the right.)	Tournez à droite.
Turn left. (literally, Turn to the left.)	Tournez à gauche.

✎ Vocabulary Practice 2

Fill in the blanks with the correct French translations. As always, feel free to use your dictionary or the glossary for help.

yes _____

no _____

It's not far. _____

It's very close./It's very near. _____

It's farther. _____

Is this the way to ... ?/Is this the direction of ... ? _____

Turn right. _____

Turn left. _____

ANSWER KEY:
oui (yes); non (no); Ce n'est pas loin. (It's not far.); C'est tout près. (It's very close./It's very near.); C'est plus loin. (It's farther.); Est-ce que c'est la direction de... ? (Is this the way to ... ?/Is this the direction of ... ?); Tournez à droite. (Turn right.); Tournez à gauche. (Turn left.)

Grammar Builder 2

▶ 6E Grammar Builder 2 (CD 2, Track 12)

You've just seen examples of questions and answers, and you've also learned some more vocabulary.

VOCABULARY FOR ASKING DIRECTIONS	
loin	*far*
près	*close (near)*
tout près	*very close (very near)*
plus loin	*farther*
ici	*here*
là	*there*
droite	*right*
gauche	*left*

You learned some vocabulary for getting around town:

VOCABULARY FOR AROUND TOWN	
la station de métro	*the metro station (the subway station)*
l'arrêt (*masc.*) de bus	*the bus stop*
la poste	*the post office*
le musée	*the museum*
la gare	*the train station*
le pont	*the bridge*

You also saw the very useful expression **il faut**, which means *you have to* or *it's necessary to* (or *you need to/you must*), as in:

Il faut traverser le pont.
You have to cross the bridge.

Allez tout droit means *go straight ahead,* and you probably recognized that **tournez** means *turn.*

Take It Further

There's one more new word to mention:

traverser	to cross, to go across

And speaking of **allez tout droit**, **allez** comes from **vous allez** (*you go*), which you first saw in Lesson 1. You actually already know several forms of *to go*:

je vais	I go
tu vas	you go (familiar)
ça va	it goes
vous allez	you go (polite/plural)

Plus, you saw **Allons-y** (*Let's go*) in Lesson 3, and **On y va** (*Let's go*) and **Comment va-t-on...** (*How do we go/get to ...*) earlier in this lesson.

You'll learn all of the forms of *to go* in Lesson 8, but as you can see, you've already gotten a pretty good head start!

✎ Work Out 1

Okay, let's put everything you've learned so far together in a short comprehension exercise. Fill in the blanks in the conversation below.

▶ 6F Work Out 1 (CD 2, Track 13). Listen to the audio to practice pronouncing the sentences below! The audio also includes the French translations, so try to complete the exercise here first before listening.

Pardon, madame, quelle est la direction pour la Cathédrale de Notre-Dame ?

Excuse me, ma'am, which way is Notre Dame Cathedral?

(literally, Excuse me, ma'am, which is the way for the Cathedral of Notre Dame?)

C'est la première rue après _____.

*It's the first street after **the bridge**.*

Est-ce que la place de la Concorde est _____ ?

*Is the Place de la Concorde **far**?*

_____ la Seine.

***Yes, you need to cross** the Seine.*

_____ pour la Tour Eiffel ?

***Which is the bus stop** for the Eiffel Tower?*

C'est l'arrêt du Champ-de-Mars.

It's the Champ-de-Mars stop.

_____ pour l'Arc de Triomphe ?

***Which is the subway station** for the Arc de Triomphe?*

C'est la station Charles-de-Gaulle(-Étoile).

It is the Charles-de-Gaulle(-Étoile) station.

_____ ?

Where is the train station?

_____ est tout droit.

***The train station** is straight ahead.*

ANSWER KEY:

le pont; loin; Oui, il faut traverser; Quel est l'arrêt de bus; Quelle est la station de métro; Où est la gare (Où se trouve la gare); La gare

Take It Further

Notice the new words pardon, après, and rue? Instead of looking at them right away, we're going to see more examples of those words in the next section, and then we'll go over each individual word.

As for première (*first*), you already know it! It's just the feminine form of the ordinal number premier (*first*), which you learned in Lesson 3. The rest of the ordinal numbers have the same form in the masculine and the feminine, except for second (*second*), which becomes seconde in the feminine.

Finally, as you have probably already figured out, while l'arrêt de bus means *bus stop*, the masculine noun arrêt on its own just means *stop*. Also:

la station	*station*
le métro	*subway, metro*
le bus	*bus*

3 Use what you've learned to get around Paris

ⓖ Bring It All Together

Now let's bring it all together and add a little bit more vocabulary and structure. Read and listen to the following dialogue of a tourist asking for directions in Paris.

▶ 6G Bring It All Together (CD 2, Track 14)

A: *Pardon me, sir, I'm lost. Where's the Champs-Elysées theater?*
**Pardon, monsieur, je suis perdue. Où se trouve le théâtre des
Champs-Élysées ?**

B: *It's the third street on the right (literally, to the right).
And it's after the avenue Montaigne.*
C'est la troisième rue à droite. Et c'est après l'avenue Montaigne.

A: *Is the Café de la Gare far from here?*
Est-ce que le Café de la Gare est loin d'ici ?

B: *No, it's very near.*
Non, c'est tout près.

A: *Which is the subway station for Sacré Cœur?*
Quelle est la station de métro pour le Sacré-Cœur ?

B: *It's Montmartre.*
C'est Montmartre.

A: *Thank you.*
Merci.

B: *You're welcome.*
De rien.
⏸

Take It Further

▶ 6H Take It Further (CD 2, Track 15)

You already knew a lot of that vocabulary, but there were a few new words, too.

perdu/perdue	lost
je suis perdu/je suis perdue	I'm lost
le théâtre	the theater
la rue	the street
l'avenue (fem.)	the avenue
le café	the café (the coffee shop, the coffee)
la troisième rue	the third street
la première rue	the first street
la deuxième rue (la seconde rue)	the second street
après	after
avant	before

You also saw some polite expressions that are useful when asking directions:

pardon	pardon (excuse me, pardon me)
merci	thank you
de rien	you're welcome, it's nothing

✎ Work Out 2

Now let's practice some of what you've learned.

▶ 6I Work Out 2 (CD 2, Track 16) for different, audio-only exercises!

Can you find the French translations of the following English phrases in the puzzle below?

1. *near*

2. *here*

3. *there*

4. *thank you*

5. *left*

6. *street*

R	É	S	U	N	I	V	E
O	P	R	È	S	M	U	D
U	R	E	S	A	E	L	O
T	O	O	Y	H	R	È	S
I	C	P	C	Ê	C	R	U
È	H	U	I	C	I	S	T
N	A	G	E	L	U	L	À
G	O	T	R	U	E	D	T

ANSWER KEY:
1. **près** (*near*); 2. **ici** (*here*); 3. **là** (*there*); 4. **merci** (*thank you*); 5. **gauche** (*left*); 6. **rue** (*street*)

✎ Drive It Home

A. Rewrite these yes/no questions using est-ce que. Remember to read each sentence aloud once you're done.

1. **Parlez-vous français ?** (*Do you speak French?*)

_____

2. **La gare est loin d'ici ?** (*Is the train station far from here?*)

_____

3. Le pont est tout près ? (*Is the bridge very close?*)

_____

4. Le théâtre est à droite ? (*Is the theater to the right?*)

_____

5. Es-tu américain ? (*Are you American?*)

_____

6. Êtes-vous perdue ? (*Are you lost?*)

_____

7. C'est la station Charles de Gaulle-Étoile ? (*Is this the Charles de Gaulle-Étoile*

   station?) _____

B. Remember how to negate sentences? You first saw how in Lesson 1, and then
   again here in Grammar Builder 1. Let's practice: negate the following sentences by
   filling in the blanks with ne... pas or n'... pas.

1. Je _____ suis _____ perdu. (*I'm not lost.*)

2. L'avenue _____ est _____ loin. (*The avenue isn't far.*)

3. Nous _____ sommes _____ américains.
   (*We aren't American.*)

4. Tu _____ parles _____ français.
   (*You don't speak French.*)

5. Vous _____ êtes _____ près de la Tour Eiffel.
   (*You're not close to the Eiffel Tower.*)

6. Je _____ comprends _____ . (*I don't understand.*)

7. La gare _____ est _____ loin d'ici.

   (*The train station isn't far from here.*)

8. Je _____ ai _____ froid. (*I'm not cold.*)

ANSWER KEY:
A: 1. Est-ce que vous parlez français ? 2. Est-ce que la gare est loin d'ici ? 3. Est-ce que le pont est tout près ? 4. Est-ce que le théâtre est à droite ? 5. Est-ce que tu es américain ? 6. Est-ce que vous êtes perdue ? 7. Est-ce que c'est la station Charles de Gaulle-Étoile ?
B: 1. ne... pas; 2. n'... pas; 3. ne... pas; 4. ne... pas; 5. n'... pas; 6. ne... pas; 7. n'... pas; 8. n'... pas

Parting Words

Congratulations!

Félicitations !

You've finished the lesson! You've learned the basic vocabulary you need to ask for directions around **une ville** (*a city*).

How did you do? You should now be able to:

☐ Ask questions (Still unsure? Go back to page 106)

☐ Ask for directions (Still unsure? Go back to page 109)

☐ Understand directions (Still unsure? Go back to page 109)

☐ Use what you've learned to get around Paris (Still unsure? Go back to page 114)

Take It Further

▶ 6K Take It Further (CD 2, Track 18)

You may of course want to extend your vocabulary a bit. Some other useful vocabulary to know is:

un magasin	*a store*
une école	*a school*
un hôpital	*a hospital*
un cinéma*	*a movie theater*
un boulevard	*a boulevard*
un supermarché	*a supermarket*
un restaurant	*a restaurant*
une boulangerie	*a bakery*
une pâtisserie	*a pastry shop*
une pharmacie	*a pharmacy (a drugstore)*

* Le cinéma can also mean *the movies*, as in *I like going to the movies.*

Ⅱ

Don't forget to go to ***www.livinglanguage.com/languagelab*** to access your free online tools for this lesson: flashcards, games, and quizzes.

Word Recall

Now let's review vocabulary from previous lessons.
Using the word bank below, translate the following English words. Some French words may not be used.

un lit	une télé
un canapé	un réfrigérateur
un livre	une voiture
une table	une douche
un jardin	un ordinateur

1. *a refrigerator* _____

2. *a TV* _____

3. *a garden* _____

4. *a shower* _____

5. *a book* _____

6. *a bed* _____

7. *a computer* _____

8. *a table* _____

ANSWER KEY:
1. un réfrigérateur; 2. une télé; 3. un jardin; 4. une douche; 5. un livre; 6. un lit; 7. un ordinateur;
8. une table

Lesson 7: At the Restaurant

Leçon sept : au restaurant

In this lesson, you'll learn how to:

1 Order at a restaurant
Name different types of food
Say *this* and *that*

2 Make a polite request

3 Use what you've learned to talk to a
waiter at a French restaurant

So, **bon appétit !** Ready for some vocabulary?

1 Order at a restaurant
Name different types of food
Say *this* and *that*

Vocabulary Builder 1

▷ 7B Vocabulary Builder 1 (CD 2, Track 20)

this restaurant	**ce restaurant**
this table	**cette table**
a fork, a knife, and a spoon	**une fourchette, un couteau et une cuillère**
the plate and the napkin	**l'assiette** (*fem.*) **et la serviette**
the menu	**la carte, le menu**
this menu	**cette carte, ce menu**
The wine list, please. (*literally, The menu/card of the wines, please.*)	**La carte des vins, s'il vous plaît.**
a dish	**un plat**
This dish is delicious.	**Ce plat est délicieux.**
the appetizer	**le hors-d'œuvre***
I'd like ... (I would like ...)	**Je voudrais...**
I'd like some soup.	**Je voudrais de la soupe.**
I'd like a drink.	**Je voudrais une boisson.**
I'd like a salad.	**Je voudrais une salade.**
some bread and some butter	**du pain et du beurre**
the salt and the pepper	**le sel et le poivre**

* Another common French word for *appetizer* is **l'entrée** (*fem.*). You'll see it on a lot of French menus. Just remember that it actually means *appetizer* and not *entrée*! Also note that you will usually see **hors-d'œuvre** in the plural: **les hors-d'œuvre** (*appetizers*).

the meat and the fish	la viande et le poisson
Chicken, beef, or pork? (literally, The chicken, the beef, or the pork?)	Le poulet, le bœuf ou le porc ?
some cheese and a dessert	du fromage et un dessert
some coffee and some tea	du café et du thé
With some sugar and some milk? (With sugar and milk?)	Avec du sucre et du lait ?

✎ Vocabulary Practice 1

Now let's practice some of the food and restaurant terms you just learned. As always, fill in the blanks with the correct French translations.

If the definite article is l', make sure to write down the gender as well.

a fork _____

a knife _____

a spoon _____

the plate _____

the napkin _____

the menu _____

the wine list_____

a dish _____

the appetizer _____

I'd like .../I would like ... _____

a drink _____

a salad _____

the salt _____

the pepper _____

the meat _____

the fish _____

the chicken _____

the beef _____

the pork _____

ANSWER KEY:

une fourchette (*a fork*); un couteau (*a knife*); une cuillère (*a spoon*); l'assiette (*fem.*) (*the plate*); la serviette (*the napkin*); la carte/le menu (*the menu*); la carte des vins (*the wine list*); un plat (*a dish*); le hors-d'œuvre/l'entrée (*fem.*) (*the appetizer*); Je voudrais... (*I'd like .../I would like ...*); une boisson (*a drink*); une salade (*a salad*); le sel (*the salt*); le poivre (*the pepper*); la viande (*the meat*); le poisson (*the fish*); le poulet (*the chicken*); le bœuf (*the beef*); le porc (*the pork*)

Grammar Builder 1

▷ 7C Grammar Builder 1 (CD 2, Track 21)

Okay, let's stop there. You've learned a lot of useful vocabulary for food and other items associated with a restaurant or with eating.

And you also learned how to say *this*. Again, gender is important. *This* is ce for masculine nouns so:

le restaurant (*the restaurant*) → ce restaurant (*this restaurant*)

This is cette for feminine nouns, so:

la table (*the table*) → cette table (*this table*)

With masculine nouns beginning with a silent h or a vowel, ce becomes cet: cet œuf (*this egg*). In the plural (*these*), it's ces: ces fromages (*these cheeses*). (Note that ces can be used with both masculine and feminine nouns.)

You also saw the very common preposition de (*of*) used in a few different ways. You can say, for example:

le goût + de + la soupe → le goût de la soupe (*the taste of the soup*)

If de is followed by le, you use du instead:

le goût + de + le plat → le goût du plat (*the taste of the dish*)

(Note that if le or la is followed by a noun beginning with a vowel or silent h, use de l' instead of du or de la: le goût de l'œuf, *the taste of the egg*.)

And when de is followed by les, you say des:

la carte + de + les vins → la carte des vins (*the wine list*, or literally, *the list or card of wines*)

The same constructions (de la, du, de l', des) can be used to mean *some*:*

du pain	some bread
de la salade	some salad
du thé	some tea
de la viande	some meat
des légumes (*masc.*)	some vegetables

* Keep in mind that des is also the plural of un/une in French. In other words, des can mean *some*, *of the*, or the plural of *a/an*.

du lait	some milk
du vin	some wine
des vins *(masc.)*	some wines

And so on.

Finally, you learned **avec** (*with*), so we can add its opposite **sans** (*without*):

du café avec du sucre
some coffee with some sugar

du thé sans lait
some tea without milk

So, to summarize:

	FEMININE	MASCULINE	MASCULINE BEFORE A VOWEL OR SILENT H
this	cette	ce	cet
these	ces	ces	ces

	FEMININE	MASCULINE	MASCULINE/ FEMININE BEFORE A VOWEL OR SILENT H
of the, some	de la	du	de l'
of the, some (plural)	des	des	des

Also remember that while *some* is often optional in English, it is usually required in French. For example, you could say either *coffee with sugar* or *some coffee with some sugar* in English, but you have to say **du café avec du sucre** in French.

Take It Further

Ce, cette, and cet actually mean both *this* and *that*. Similarly, ces means both *these* and *those*.

If you want to emphasize that you mean *that* and not *this*, or vice versa, you can use two words that you're already familiar with: -ci (*here*) and -là (*there*). Just add them after the noun. For example, you could say:

| cette table-ci | *this table (here)* |
| cette table-là | *that table (there)* |

You could also say:

| ces tables-ci | *these tables (here)* |
| ces tables-là | *those tables (there)* |

You may have noticed the word au in the title of this lesson: au restaurant (*at the restaurant*). You just learned that de + le forms du (*of the, some*). Well, it's a similar situation with the word à, which as you know means *to, at,* or *in*. In other words:

à + le = au

à + la = à la

à + l' = à l'

à + les = aux

So au restaurant is actually à + le restaurant (*at the restaurant*).

Je voudrais (*I would like*), as you can imagine, is a very useful phrase to know whenever you need something. The phrase is actually a "conditional" form of the verb **vouloir** (*to want*). You'll learn more about the conditional if you bought *Complete French* and choose to continue on after this book.

Finally, if you're a little confused about all of the different words for *this, that,* and *of the*, don't worry. You'll have a chance to practice them in Work Out 2 and Drive It Home.

2 Make a polite request

Vocabulary Builder 2

▶ 7D Vocabulary Builder 2 (CD 2, Track 22)

I'd like a table for two, please.	**Je voudrais une table pour deux, s'il vous plaît.**
Give me the menu, please.	**Donnez-moi le menu (la carte), s'il vous plaît.**
Have you chosen?	**Vous avez choisi ?**
To start?	**Pour commencer ?**
Bring me some bread, please.	**Apportez-moi du pain, s'il vous plaît.**
Give me these appetizers, please.	**Donnez-moi ces hors-d'œuvre, s'il vous plaît.**
Bring me this drink, please.	**Apportez-moi cette boisson, s'il vous plaît.**
And for dessert?	**Et pour le dessert ?**

Show me these pastries, please.	Montrez-moi ces pâtisseries, s'il vous plaît.
Give me a coffee with cream, please.	Donnez-moi un café-crème, s'il vous plaît.
Bring me the check, please.	Apportez-moi l'addition, s'il vous plaît.

✎ Vocabulary Practice 2

Fill in the blanks with the correct French translations. If the article is l', make sure to include the gender as well. (Hint: the French words for *pastry* and *check* are feminine.)

a table for two _____

the pastry _____

a coffee with cream _____

the check _____

ANSWER KEY:
une table pour deux (*a table for two*); la pâtisserie (*the pastry*); un café-crème (*a coffee with cream*); l'addition (*fem.*) (*the check*)

Grammar Builder 2

▶ 7E Grammar Builder 2 (CD 2, Track 23)

Let's pause there for a moment.

You've already seen the polite request je voudrais (*I'd like*), which of course is often used with s'il vous plaît (*please*). You could also simply say je veux (*I want*). (Although that isn't as polite.)

Other ways to ask for things are to say:

apportez-moi	*bring me*
donnez-moi	*give me*

Notice that these command forms end in -ez. Another example of this was:

montrez-moi	*show me*

Take It Further

You now know two forms of the verb vouloir (to want):

je veux	*I want*
vous voulez	*you want (polite/plural)*

Plus a conditional form: je voudrais (*I would like*). You'll learn more (non-conditional) forms of the verb in Lesson 10, but you're already off to a great start!

You were also introduced to the past tense of the verb choisir (*to choose*) in the phrase:

Vous avez choisi ?

Have you chosen?

Vous avez, as you know, means *you have*. However, it is also used in French to form the past tense, as it is in English (***Have you*** *chosen?*). You'll learn more about the past tense if you bought *Complete French* and are continuing on to *Intermediate French*.

As an additional note, you learned in Lesson 6 that une pâtisserie meant *a pastry shop*. However, as you saw in this lesson, it can also mean *a pastry*.

✎ Work Out 1

Okay, let's put everything you've learned so far together in a short comprehension exercise. Fill in the appropriate polite requests in the conversation below.

▶ 7F Work Out 1 (CD 2, Track 24). Listen to the audio to practice pronouncing the sentences below! The audio also includes the French translations, so try to complete the exercise here first before listening.

Mademoiselle, _____. Quelles sont les spécialités du jour ?

Les crudités, qu'est-ce que c'est ?

*Miss, **bring me the menu, please**. What are the specialties of the day? What are*

crudités? (literally, Crudités, what is that?)

Des légumes crus, surtout des radis.

Raw vegetables, mostly radishes.

_____ .

Bring me the fish, please.

Et pour le dessert, monsieur ?

And for dessert, sir?

_____ les fromages, les pâtisseries et les fruits, _____ .

_____ . Avec du sucre et du lait.

***Show me** the cheeses, pastries, and fruit, **please. Give me a coffee, please**. With*

some sugar and some milk.

And at the end of the meal:

Bring me the check, please.

ANSWER KEY:

apportez-moi la carte/le menu, s'il vous plaît; Apportez-moi le poisson, s'il vous plaît; Montrez-moi; s'il vous plaît; Donnez-moi un café, s'il vous plaît; Apportez-moi l'addition, s'il vous plaît

Take It Further

Notice some new words? Let's review:

surtout	_mostly, above all, especially_
la spécialité	_the specialty_
le jour	_the day_
les crudités (_fem._)	_the crudités – a French appetizer of raw, mixed vegetables_
cru/crue	_raw_
le radis	_the radish_
le fruit	_the fruit_

Remember qu'est-ce que c'est ? from the previous lesson? It means _what is it/this/that?_ or _what are they/these/those?_. It can be a very helpful expression to know if you're in a store or at a restaurant and you're unsure of what something is. Just indicate the item or phrase on the menu and politely say: Qu'est-ce que c'est ?

3 Use what you've learned to talk to a waiter at a French restaurant

ⓐ Bring It All Together

Now let's bring it all together and add a little bit more vocabulary and structure.
Read and listen to the following dialogue at a restaurant, as two customers reserve
a table, order, and get the check.

▶ 7G Bring It All Together (CD 2, Track 25)

A: *I'd like to reserve a table, please.*
Je voudrais réserver une table, s'il vous plaît.

B: *Bring me the menu, please.*
Apportez-moi le menu, s'il vous plaît.

C: *To start, madam, some appetizers?*
Pour commencer, madame, des hors-d'œuvre ?

B: *Give me some homemade pâté.*
Donnez-moi du pâté maison.

A: *And a bottle of red wine, too.*
Et une bouteille de vin rouge, aussi.

B: *I'd like this onion soup.*
Je voudrais cette soupe à l'oignon.

A: *Bring me this duck à l'orange.*
Apportez-moi ce canard à l'orange.

C: *And for dessert?*
Et pour le dessert ?

A: *Some Crêpes Suzette.*
Des crêpes Suzette.

B: *Give me the check, please.*
Donnez-moi l'addition, s'il vous plaît.

Take It Further

You already knew a lot of that vocabulary, but there were a few new words, too:

réserver	*to reserve*
le pâté	*the pâté* – a spreadable purée of meat
une bouteille	*a bottle*
la soupe à l'oignon	*the onion soup*
l'oignon (*masc.*)	*the onion*
le canard à l'orange	*the duck à l'orange, the duck with orange sauce*
le canard	*the duck*
l'orange (*fem.*)	*the orange*
la crêpe Suzette	*the Crêpe Suzette* – a crêpe with sugar, orange, and liqueur
la crêpe	*the crêpe* – a tissue-thin pancake

Finally, you already knew that la maison meant *house* or *home*, but now you know that maison can also be used as an adjective to mean *homemade*.

Work Out 2

7H Work Out 2 (CD 2, Track 26) for different, audio-only exercises! You'll practice talking about food and dishes like **une quiche lorraine**, which is a type of quiche made with bacon.

In this lesson, you learned how to combine **de** and **à** with the definite articles (**le, la, l', les**). Now let's practice what you learned by filling in the blanks below.

1. de + le = _____

2. de + la = _____

3. de + l' = _____

4. de + les = _____

5. à + le = _____

6. à + la = _____

7. à + l' = _____

8. à + les = _____

ANSWER KEY:
1. du; 2. de la; 3. de l'; 4. des; 5. au; 6. à la; 7. à l'; 8. aux

Drive It Home

A. Fill in the blanks with **du** or **de la**. Don't forget to read each sentence aloud once you're done. Ready?

1. Je voudrais _____ lait, s'il vous plaît.

   (*I'd like some milk, please.*)

2. Je voudrais _____ sucre, s'il vous plaît.

   (*I'd like some sugar, please.*)

3. Je voudrais _____ poulet, s'il vous plaît.

   (*I'd like some chicken, please.*)

4. Je voudrais _____ soupe, s'il vous plaît.

(*I'd like some soup, please.*)

5. Je voudrais _____ thé, s'il vous plaît.

(*I'd like some tea, please.*)

6. Je voudrais _____ sel, s'il vous plaît.

(*I'd like some salt, please.*)

7. Je voudrais _____ café, s'il vous plaît.

(*I'd like some coffee, please.*)

8. Je voudrais _____ salade, s'il vous plaît.

(*I'd like some salad, please.*)

B. Now fill in the blanks with ce or cette. Ready?

1. Apportez-moi _____ pâtisserie, s'il vous plaît.

(*Bring me this/that pastry, please.*)

2. Apportez-moi _____ pain, s'il vous plaît.

(*Bring me this/that bread, please.*)

3. Apportez-moi _____ soupe, s'il vous plaît.

(*Bring me this/that soup, please.*)

4. Apportez-moi _____ spécialité, s'il vous plaît.

(*Bring me this/that specialty, please.*)

5. Apportez-moi _____ fromage, s'il vous plaît.

(*Bring me this/that cheese, please.*)

6. Apportez-moi _____ viande, s'il vous plaît.

   (Bring me this/that meat, please.)

7. Apportez-moi _____ vin, s'il vous plaît.

   (Bring me this/that wine, please.)

8. Apportez-moi _____ dessert, s'il vous plaît.

   (Bring me this/that dessert, please.)

ANSWER KEY:
A: 1. du; 2. du; 3. du; 4. de la; 5. du; 6. du; 7. du; 8. de la
B: 1. cette; 2. ce; 3. cette; 4. cette; 5. ce; 6. cette; 7. ce; 8. ce

Parting Words

Congratulations!

Félicitations !

You've finished the lesson! How did you do? You should now be able to:

☐ Order at a restaurant (Still unsure? Go back to page 123)

☐ Name different types of food (Still unsure? Go back to page 123)

☐ Say *this* and *that* (Still unsure? Go back to page 125)

☐ Make a polite request (Still unsure? Go back to page 130)

☐ Use what you've learned to talk to a waiter at a French restaurant
   (Still unsure? Go back to page 134)

Take It Further

▶ 7J Take It Further (CD 2, Track 28)

You may of course want to extend your vocabulary a bit. Here are some other well-known **hors-d'œuvre:**

les sardines (*fem.*) sauce tomate	the sardines in tomato sauce
le melon	the melon

Some other *dishes*, or **plats,** are:

le consommé aux vermicelles	the noodle soup
la bisque de homard	the lobster bisque
la côte de porc	the pork chop
le carré d'agneau rôti	the roast rack of lamb
la truite au bleu	the trout cooked in wine (*and vinegar*)
le rôti de bœuf	the roast beef

Side dishes include:

le riz	the rice

And **des légumes** (*some vegetables*) like:

les haricots (*masc.*) verts	the green beans
les pommes (*fem.*) de terre	the potatoes

(Another popular side dish is **les frites** [*fem.*], or *the French fries.*)

Red, white and *rosé wines* are:

le vin rouge	*the red wine*
le vin blanc	*the white wine*
le (vin) rosé*	*the rosé wine*

* When talking about *rosé wine*, the word vin is often dropped.

For dessert, you might want to try:

la pêche Melba	*the peaches with ice cream*
la salade de fruits	*the fruit salad*
la mousse au chocolat	*the chocolate mousse*
la crème caramel	*the creamy dessert made with caramel*

And remember, if you just order un café (in France), you'll get a black coffee. If you want cream in your coffee, order un café-crème.

Bon appétit !

Don't forget to go to *www.livinglanguage.com/languagelab* to access your free online tools for this lesson: flashcards, games, and quizzes.

Word Recall

Now let's review vocabulary from previous lessons.

A. First, let's practice family vocabulary. Fill in the following family tree with the correct French word for each member of the family. Make sure to include **le**, **la**, or **l'** before each French word.

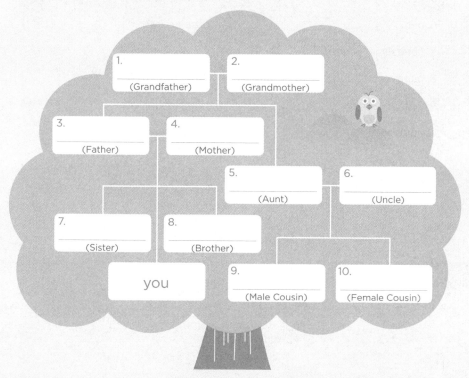

1. _____ (Grandfather)
2. _____ (Grandmother)
3. _____ (Father)
4. _____ (Mother)
5. _____ (Aunt)
6. _____ (Uncle)
7. _____ (Sister)
8. _____ (Brother)

you

9. _____ (Male Cousin)
10. _____ (Female Cousin)

B. Now match the English adjectives on the left to the correct French translations on the right:

1. *big*		a. **mauvais/mauvaise**	
2. *small*		b. **nouveau/nouvelle**	
3. *good*		c. **amusant/amusante**	
4. *bad*		d. **petit/petite**	
5. *new*		e. **cher/chère**	
6. *old*		f. **beau/belle**	
7. *handsome, beautiful*		g. **bon/bonne**	
8. *happy*		h. **vieux/vieille**	
9. *dear, expensive*		i. **grand/grande**	
10. *amusing*		j. **heureux/heureuse**	

ANSWER KEY:

A: 1. le grand-père (*the grandfather*); 2. la grand-mère (*the grandmother*); 3. le père (*the father*); 4. la mère (*the mother*); 5. la tante (*the aunt*); 6. l'oncle (*the uncle*); 7. la sœur (*the sister*); 8. le frère (*the brother*); 9. le cousin (*the male cousin*); 10. la cousine (*the female cousin*)

B: 1. i; 2. d; 3. g; 4. a; 5. b; 6. h; 7. f; 8. j; 9. e; 10. c

At the Restaurant

At Work

Review Dialogues

round Town

Everyday Life

Socializing

Lesson 8: Everyday Life

Leçon huit : la vie quotidienne

In this lesson, you'll learn some common verbs so you can talk about everyday life. You'll learn how to:

1 Talk about different actions in the present
Talk about doing something *yourself*

2 Say what you *do*, where you *go*, and what you *take*

3 Use what you've learned to describe what you do every day

First, let's get started with typical activities of your daily routine.

1 Talk about different actions in the present
Talk about doing something *yourself*

Vocabulary Builder 1

▶ 8B Vocabulary Builder 1 (CD 2, Track 30)

I get up.	Je me lève.
I wash up.	Je me lave.
I have my breakfast. (literally, I take my breakfast.)	Je prends mon petit déjeuner.
I get dressed.	Je m'habille.
I go to the office.	Je vais au bureau.
I go to school. (literally, I go to the school.)	Je vais à l'école.
I work a lot.	Je travaille beaucoup.
I have lunch.	Je déjeune.
I go home.	Je rentre à la maison.
I watch television.	Je regarde la télé.
I read a book.	Je lis un livre.
I go to bed.	Je me couche.

✎ Vocabulary Practice 1

Now let's practice what you just learned. As always, fill in the blanks with the correct French translations.

I wash up _____

I have my breakfast _____

I get dressed _____

I go to the office _____

I go to school _____

I go home _____

I watch television _____

I read a book _____

I go to bed _____

ANSWER KEY:

Je me lave (*I wash up*); Je prends mon petit déjeuner (*I have my breakfast*); Je m'habille (*I get dressed*); Je vais au bureau (*I go to the office*); Je vais à l'école (*I go to school*); Je rentre à la maison (*I go home*); Je regarde la télé (*I watch television*); Je lis un livre (*I read a book*); Je me couche (*I go to bed*)

Grammar Builder 1

8C Grammar Builder 1 (CD 2, Track 31)

Verbs are an important part of any language, and they're also usually difficult to master. We're not going to go into a lot of detail about French verbs in this program, but you'll learn enough of the basics so that you can get started using them.

Verbs in French are conjugated, which means that they change forms slightly depending on the subject. The basic form of a verb is its infinitive, which is just like the *to* form in English (*to speak, to work, to have,* etc.).

French infinitives have a few different endings, but the most common is -er, pronounced [ay]. So, for example:

travailler	to work
déjeuner	to have lunch
rentrer	to go home*

* So does Je rentre à la maison mean *I go home to the home*? Well, rentrer can also be translated as *to return, to come back (in)*, or *to go in*. As a result, sometimes the phrase à la maison is added for clarification.

And so on.

To conjugate these verbs in the je (*I*) form, the -er ending is replaced by just -e, which is silent, and gives you:

je travaille	zhuh trah-vahy	I work
je déjeune	zhuh day-zhuhn	I have lunch
je rentre	zhuh rah(n)-truh	I go home

(Note the phonetics provided, but don't forget to listen to the audio to get a better sense of the pronunciation!)

Try that now with regarder (*to watch*). Can you think of the je form?

It's je regarde (*I watch*).

If you know the je form of an -er ending verb like these, you automatically know the tu (*you, familiar*), il or elle (*he or she*), and ils or elles (*they*) forms. They're spelled differently, but they're all pronounced just like the je forms.

tu regardes	tew ruh-gahrd	you watch (*familiar*)
il rentre	eel rah(n)-truh	he goes home

| elle travaille | ehl trah-vahy | she works |
| ils travaillent | eel trah-vahy | they work (masc.) |

In spelling, the **tu** form ends in **-es**, the **il** and **elle** forms end in **-e**, just like the **je** form, and the **ils** and **elles** forms end in **-ent**, which is completely silent. But they're all pronounced the same:

TRAVAILLER *(TO WORK)*		
je travaille	zhuh trah-vahy	*I work*
tu travailles	tew trah-vahy	*you work (familiar)*
il travaille	eel trah-vahy	*he works*
elle travaille	ehl trah-vahy	*she works*
ils travaillent	eel trah-vahy	*they work (masc.)*
elles travaillent	ehl trah-vahy	*they work (fem.)*

The missing forms are the **nous** (*we*) and **vous** (*you, polite* or *plural*) forms. For **nous**, add **-ons**, pronounced [oh(n)]. And for **vous**, add **-ez**, which is pronounced [ay], just like the *to* infinitive form. So:

TRAVAILLER *(TO WORK)*		
nous travaillons	noo trah vah-yoh(n)	*we work*
vous travaillez	voo trah-vah-yay	*you work (polite/plural)*

Now, let's do the whole thing with another common verb, **parler** (*to speak*). Ready?

PARLER *(TO SPEAK)*	
je parle	*I speak*
tu parles	*you speak (familiar)*
il parle*	*he speaks*
elle parle	*she speaks*

* Remember that **on** (*we, one, people in general*) uses the same form as **il** and **elle**. So: **on parle, on travaille**, etc.

PARLER *(TO SPEAK)*	
nous parlons	*we speak*
vous parlez	*you speak (polite/plural)*
ils parlent	*they speak (masc.)*
elles parlent	*they speak (fem.)*

And that is how to conjugate a verb in French!

You may have noticed that some of the verbs in the examples you saw in Vocabulary Builder 1 have a little me (or m') before them:

je me lève	*I get up*
je me lave	*I wash up*
je m'habille	*I get dressed*
je me couche	*I go to bed*

These are, in technical terms, called "reflexive verbs," and French has a lot of them. All that means is that they're conjugated with an extra pronoun, in this case, me (or m' before a silent h or vowel), which can be thought of as meaning *myself.*

So, je me lève (literally) means something like *I lift myself out of bed.* And:

je me lave	*I wash myself*
je m'habille	*I dress myself*
je me couche	*I put myself in bed*

In the infinitive, the pronoun is se (or s' before a silent h or vowel), so se laver means *to wash oneself.* That pronoun is also used with *he, she,* and *they,* so:

il se couche	*he goes to bed (literally, he puts himself in bed)*
elle s'habille	*she gets dressed (literally, she dresses herself)*

And so on (ils se lavent, elles se lèvent, etc.).

(Note that se is used with the pronoun on as well: on se couche.)

With tu, use te (or t'):

tu te lèves	you get up (literally, you lift yourself out of bed)

Nous and vous are easy; just use the same pronoun twice.

nous nous lavons	we wash up (literally, we wash ourselves)
vous vous habillez	you get dressed (literally, you dress yourself/yourselves)

Finally, even though most French verbs end in -er in the infinitive form and are conjugated like parler (to speak) or travailler (to work), there are some verbs that end in -ir, like finir (to finish), some that end in -re like prendre (to take), and plenty of irregulars, like être (to be) and avoir (to have), which you've already learned.

You could spend a lot of time on French verbs, but in this program we're just going to cover enough of the basics to get you started.

Take It Further

You've actually seen a reflexive verb before: je m'appelle, tu t'appelles, and vous vous appelez are all forms of the reflexive verb s'appeler (to be called). Here is its full conjugation:

S'APPELER (TO BE CALLED)	
je m'appelle	I am called
tu t'appelles	you are called (familiar)

S'APPELER *(TO BE CALLED)*	
il s'appelle	*he is called*
elle s'appelle	*she is called*
nous nous appelons	*we are called*
vous vous appelez	*you are called (polite/plural)*
ils s'appellent	*they are called (masc.)*
elles s'appellent	*they are called (fem.)*

Notice that s'appeler is an -er verb, but it actually conjugates slightly irregularly: it doubles the l in every form except for nous and vous. Otherwise, it is formed like any other -er verb.

Another reflexive verb that's slightly irregular is se lever *(to get up)*:

SE LEVER *(TO GET UP)*	
je me lève	*I get up*
tu te lèves	*you get up (familiar)*
il se lève	*he gets up*
elle se lève	*she gets up*
nous nous levons	*we get up*
vous vous levez	*you get up (polite/plural)*
ils se lèvent	*they get up (masc.)*
elles se lèvent	*they get up (fem.)*

Notice that the first e changes to an è in every form except for nous and vous.

Fortunately, s'habiller *(to get dressed)*, se coucher *(to go to bed)*, and se laver *(to wash oneself, to wash up)* conjugate just like any other -er verb, plus the extra pronoun.

You also saw examples of these verbs in Vocabulary Builder 1:

| lire | to read |
| prendre | to take, to have |

Je lis is the je form of lire, and je prends is the je form of prendre. As was noted in Grammar Builder 1, prendre is an -re verb, but it's actually an irregular -re verb. You'll learn its full conjugation in Grammar Builder 2.

Lire is also an -re verb and it's also irregular. Its full conjugation is as follows:

LIRE (TO READ)	
je lis	I read
tu lis	you read (familiar)
il lit	he reads
elle lit	she reads
nous lisons	we read
vous lisez	you read (polite/plural)
ils lisent	they read (masc.)
elles lisent	they read (fem.)

2 Say what you *do*, where you *go*, and what you *take*

Vocabulary Builder 2
8D Vocabulary Builder 2 (CD 2, Track 32)

I do the house cleaning.	Je fais le ménage.
You do the cooking.	Tu fais la cuisine.
He does the shopping.	Il fait les courses.

She consults the doctor.	Elle consulte le médecin.
We have fun.	Nous nous amusons.
You go to the movies. *(You go to the movie theater.)*	Vous allez au cinéma.
They go to the theater.	Ils vont au théâtre.
Pierre and Louis go to the soccer stadium.	Pierre et Louis vont au stade de foot.
I take a vacation.	Je prends des vacances.*
We take the train.	Nous prenons le train.

* Although singular in English, *vacation* is always plural in French: les vacances (*the vacation*), des vacances (*a vacation*), etc. It's a feminine plural noun.

✎ Vocabulary Practice 2

Fill in the blanks with the correct French translations. As always, feel free to use a dictionary or the glossary if you need to.

the doctor _____

the movies, the movie theater _____

the theater _____

the soccer stadium _____

a vacation _____

the train _____

ANSWER KEY:
le médecin (*the doctor*); le cinéma (*the movies, the movie theater*); le théâtre (*the theater*); le stade de foot (*the soccer stadium*); des vacances (*a vacation*); le train (*the train*)

Grammar Builder 2

8E Grammar Builder 2 (CD 2, Track 33)

Let's pause.

You've seen two important irregular verbs in that list: faire (*to do*) and aller (*to go*).

The full conjugation of faire is:

FAIRE *(TO DO)*	
je fais	*I do*
tu fais	*you do (familiar)*
il fait	*he does*
elle fait	*she does*
nous faisons	*we do*
vous faites	*you do (polite/plural)*
ils font	*they do (masc.)*
elles font	*they do (fem.)*

Aller (*to go*) is also irregular. Its forms are:

ALLER *(TO GO)*	
je vais	*I go*
tu vas	*you go (familiar)*
il va*	*he goes*
elle va	*she goes*
nous allons	*we go*
vous allez	*you go (polite/plural)*
ils vont	*they go (masc.)*
elles vont	*they go (fem.)*

* Remember ça va? Since ça and il/elle can both mean *it*, ça uses the same form as il/elle: va.

You also saw prendre (*to take*), whose forms are:

PRENDRE *(TO TAKE)*	
je prends	*I take*
tu prends	*you take (familiar)*
il prend	*he takes*
elle prend	*she takes*
nous prenons	*we take*
vous prenez	*you take (polite/plural)*
ils prennent	*they take (masc.)*
elles prennent	*they take (fem.)*

These three verbs are good irregular verbs to know, since they come up very often in French. Practice them by reading and listening to their forms and repeating them until you're comfortable.

Also, go back over the examples you saw in Vocabulary Builder 2 and change the subjects. For example, instead of saying nous prenons le train (*we take the train*), say:

je prends le train
I take the train

or

elles prennent le train
they take the train

Take It Further

Just one additional verb to mention:

consulter	to consult

Consulter is a regular **-er** verb, so it follows the same pattern as other **-er** verbs: **je consulte**, **tu consultes**, etc.

You also saw the phrase **nous nous amusons** (*we have fun*) in Vocabulary Builder 2. As you can probably guess, it's the **nous** form of a reflexive verb. You'll learn more about it later on in the lesson.

✎ Work Out 1

Let's practice what you've learned. Translate the following text as best you can, using the word bank below to help you.

rester	to stay
puis	then
parfois	sometimes
ensemble	together
le week-end	the weekend, over the weekend, on the weekend
le travail	work
un taxi	a taxi

▶ 8F Work Out 1 (CD 2, Track 34). Listen to the audio to practice pronouncing the following sentences! The audio also includes the English translations, so try to translate the text below first before listening.

Michel et Julie se lèvent, et puis ils se lavent. Ils vont au bureau. Michel prend le bus, et Julie prend le métro. Après le travail, ils rentrent à la maison. Michel et Julie font les courses. Ils vont au supermarché. Ils prennent un taxi.

Le week-end, ils restent à la maison. Julie fait la cuisine et Michel fait le ménage. Puis ils regardent la télé ensemble. Parfois, ils vont au cinéma.

ANSWER KEY:

Michel and Julie get up, and then they wash up/wash themselves. They go to the office. Michel takes the bus, and Julie takes the subway/metro. After work, they go home. Michel and Julie do the shopping (go shopping). They go to the supermarket. They take a taxi.

Over/On the weekend, they stay at home. Julie does the cooking and Michel does the house cleaning. Then they watch television/TV together. Sometimes, they go to the movies/the movie theater.

Take It Further

Good job! Isn't it amazing how much you already know? You can already translate two full paragraphs about everyday life!

3 Use what you've learned to describe what you do every day

Bring It All Together

Now let's bring it all together and add a little bit more vocabulary and structure. Read and listen to the following monologue describing the activities of friends and family.

▶ 8G Bring It All Together (CD 2, Track 35)

Robert gets up.
Robert se lève.

You go to school.
Tu vas à l'école.

Henri has fun at recess.
Henri s'amuse à la récréation.

I go home.
Je rentre à la maison.

Marlène does her homework.
Marlène fait ses devoirs.

We watch TV.
Nous regardons la télé.

Paul goes to bed.
Paul se couche.

Rémy visits the museum.
Rémy visite le musée.

Odile buys clothes at the store.
Odile achète des vêtements au magasin.

You buy stamps at the post office.
Tu achètes des timbres à la poste.

You wait in line.
Tu fais la queue.

Take It Further

8H Take It Further (CD 2, Track 36)

Okay, you already knew a lot of that vocabulary, but there were a few new words, too:

acheter*	to buy
visiter	to visit (a place)
s'amuser (reflexive verb)	to have fun

* Note that acheter conjugates like se lever, minus the extra reflexive pronoun of course. You'll learn more if you bought *Complete French* and are continuing on after this course. Also, remember nous nous amusons? Now you know the infinitive form: s'amuser. It's a regular -er reflexive verb.

Other words that will come in handy in everyday life are:

la récréation (la récré)	recess
les devoirs *(masc.)*	homework
les vêtements *(masc.)*	clothes
le magasin	store
les timbres *(masc.)*	stamps

The expression faire la queue means *to wait in line.* (Or literally, *to do the line.*)

✎ Work Out 2

8I Work Out 2 (CD 3, Track 1) for different, audio-only exercises!

Let's practice conjugating irregular verbs. If you feel unclear about any of the verbs you saw in Grammar Builder 2, you may want to first go back and review.

Fill in the crossword with the correct French conjugations based on the pronoun and infinitive provided. For example, if you saw [tu, faire], you would write fais in the crossword.

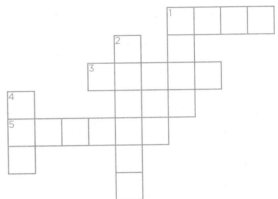

ACROSS

1 je, faire

3 elle, prendre

5 nous, aller

DOWN

1 elles, faire

2 vous, prendre

4 tu, aller

ANSWER KEY:

Across: 1. fais; 3. prend; 5. allons Down: 1. font; 2. prenez; 4. vas

✎ Drive It Home

A. Fill in the blanks with the correct form of the verb regarder (*to watch*), and then read each sentence aloud.

1. Je _____ la télé. (*I watch TV.*)

2. Tu _____ la télé. (*You watch TV.*)

3. Il _____ la télé. (*He watches TV.*)

4. Elle _____ la télé. (*She watches TV.*)

5. Nous _____ la télé. (*We watch TV.*)

6. Vous _____ la télé. (*You watch TV.*)

7. Ils _____ la télé. (*They watch TV.*)

8. Elles _____ la télé. (*They watch TV.*)

B. Great! Now complete the following sentences with the appropriate reflexive pronoun.

1. Je _____ amuse. (*I have fun.*)

2. Tu _____ amuses. (*You have fun.*)

3. Il _____ amuse. (*He has fun.*)

4. Elle _____ amuse. (*She has fun.*)

5. Nous _____ amusons. (*We have fun.*)

6. Vous _____ amusez. (*You have fun.*)

7. Ils _____ amusent. (*They have fun.*)

8. Elles _____ amusent. (*They have fun.*)

ANSWER KEY:
A: 1. regarde; 2. regardes; 3. regarde; 4. regarde; 5. regardons; 6. regardez; 7. regardent; 8. regardent
B: 1. m'; 2. t'; 3. s'; 4. s'; 5. nous; 6. vous; 7. s'; 8. s'

Parting Words

Congratulations!
Félicitations !

You've finished the lesson! You've learned the basic vocabulary you need to describe a few aspects of your everyday life. You've also learned a lot about using verbs in French.

How did you do? You should now be able to:

☐ Talk about different actions in the present (Still unsure? Go back to page 145)

☐ Talk about doing something *yourself* (Still unsure? Go back to page 148)

☐ Say what you *do*, where you *go*, and what you *take*
(Still unsure? Go back to page 153)

☐ Use what you've learned to describe what you do every day
(Still unsure? Go back to page 157)

Take It Further

▶ 8K Take It Further (CD 3, Track 3)

Some other **-er** verbs that may come in handy are:

étudier	*to study*
penser	*to think*
manger	*to eat*
payer	*to pay*
aimer	*to love, to like*
arriver	*to arrive (to get somewhere, to reach)*
entrer	*to enter, to come in*
célébrer	*to celebrate*
chercher	*to look for*
écouter	*to listen (to)*
voyager	*to travel*
commencer	*to begin (to start)*
téléphoner	*to phone (to call, to make a phone call)*
demander	*to ask*
détester	*to hate*
donner	*to give*
fermer	*to close*
habiter	*to live*
inviter	*to invite*

jouer	to play
chanter	to sing
montrer	to show
porter	to carry, to wear
présenter	to introduce
décider	to decide
trouver	to find
terminer	to finish

They all follow the same pattern as the regular -er verbs you've learned in this lesson (with some exceptions, such as manger and payer, that you'll learn more about if you bought *Complete French* and choose to continue past this book).

Don't forget that to say that you *don't* do something, just use ne (n') and pas around the verb:

je ne chante pas	I don't sing
ils ne voyagent pas beaucoup	they don't travel a lot
nous n'habitons pas ici	we don't live here

If you want to review this lesson to really master the basics of French verbs, go right ahead!

(II)

Don't forget to go to *www.livinglanguage.com/languagelab* to access your free online tools for this lesson: flashcards, games, and quizzes.

Word Recall

Now let's review vocabulary from previous lessons. Ready?

A. Translate the following numbers into French:

1. *eight* _____

2. *thirty-one* _____

3. *fifty-seven* _____

4. *ninety* _____

5. *ninety-two* _____

6. *one hundred* _____

7. *sixty* _____

8. *seventy-one* _____

9. *one thousand* _____

10. *thirteen* _____

B. Fill in the table below by placing each of the following words in the appropriate box, and then translating it into English. Each box will have four words once completed.

le poulet, le vin, les pommes de terre, le porc, le poivre, le thé, le riz, le beurre, le sucre, le bœuf, le lait, le canard, les haricots verts, le café, les frites, le sel

Hot/Cold Drinks	
Meats	
Side Dishes	
Condiments/Seasonings	

Lesson 9: At Work

Leçon neuf : au travail

In this lesson, you'll learn vocabulary related to your work life. You'll learn how to:

1 Talk about different professions

2 Say the days of the week
Tell time

3 Use what you've learned to discuss professions and schedules

And we'll go over negation with ne... pas again. Ready?

1 Talk about different professions

Vocabulary Builder 1

▶ 9B Vocabulary Builder 1 (CD 3, Track 5)

The doctor practices medicine.	Le médecin pratique la médecine.
The artist paints paintings.	L'artiste peint des tableaux.
A lawyer is speaking with a client.	Une avocate parle avec un client.
The actor plays roles.	L'acteur joue des rôles.
A cook cooks (prepares) dishes.	Un cuisinier prépare des plats.
The singer sings songs.	La chanteuse chante des chansons.
The writer writes books.	L'écrivain écrit des livres.
The soccer player plays matches.	Le footballeur joue des matches.
The manager organizes a meeting.	La gérante organise une réunion.

✎ Vocabulary Practice 1

Now let's practice what you just learned.

Make sure to include the appropriate definite article (le, la, l', les) before the French word for *medicine*. (Hint: the French words for *role* and *match* are masculine and the French word for *song* is feminine.)

medicine _____

a role _____

a song _____

a (sports) match _____

a meeting _____

ANSWER KEY:
la médecine (*medicine*); un rôle (*a role*); une chanson (*a song*); un match (*a [sports] match*); une réunion (*a meeting*)

Grammar Builder 1

9C Grammar Builder 1 (CD 3, Track 6)

You probably noticed that the names of professions have different forms for different genders. Sometimes just the article changes, as in:

| un artiste/une artiste | *an artist (male/female)* |

Sometimes an -e is added to the masculine to form the feminine, as in:

le professeur/la professeure*	*the teacher (male/female)*
le gérant/la gérante	*the manager (male/female)*
un avocat/une avocate	*a lawyer (male/female)*

* As you've probably guessed, professeur/professeure can also mean *professor*. Also note that, in casual conversation, professeur/professeure is often shortened to just prof. Furthermore, le professeur is sometimes used to refer to a *female teacher/professor* since the word la professeure is relatively new.

There are also a few common patterns of changes to word endings:

le chanteur/la chanteuse	*the singer (male/female)*
un acteur/une actrice	*an actor/actress*
le cuisinier/la cuisinière	*the cook (male/female)*

A few professions don't change at all:

| le médecin | *the male/female doctor* |
| un écrivain* | *a male/female writer* |

* Although occasionally you do see une écrivaine for *a female writer*.

Take It Further

Other professions and roles mentioned in Vocabulary Builder 1 include:

| le client/la cliente | the client (male/female) |
| le footballeur/la footballeuse | the soccer player (male/female) |

Notice that footballeur/footballeuse follows the same pattern as chanteur/chanteuse.

You also saw some new verbs related to professions:

pratiquer	to practice, to play
peindre	to paint
préparer	to prepare, to make, to cook
écrire	to write
organiser	to organize

Another good verb to know when talking about professions is:

| enseigner | to teach |

And to review, you first saw these verbs at the end of Lesson 8 and then again in Vocabulary Builder 1:

| jouer | to play, to perform, to act |
| chanter | to sing |

2 Say the days of the week
Tell time

Vocabulary Builder 2

Notice that the days of the week are not capitalized in French. The same is true for the months of the year, as you'll see later on in this lesson.

▶ 9D Vocabulary Builder 2 (CD 3, Track 7)

Monday, Tuesday, Wednesday	lundi, mardi, mercredi
Thursday, Friday	jeudi, vendredi
Saturday, Sunday	samedi, dimanche
What time is it? *(literally, What hour is it?)*	Quelle heure est-il ?*
It's 1:00.	Il est une heure.
It's half past two.	Il est deux heures et demie.
It's a quarter after four.	Il est quatre heures et quart.
It's a quarter to seven.	Il est sept heures moins le quart.
It's noon.	Il est midi.
It's midnight.	Il est minuit.

Ⅱ   * Note that the word heure (*hour*) is feminine: quelle heure, une heure.

✎ Vocabulary Practice 2

Fill in the blanks with the correct French translations. Remember that the days of the week are not capitalized in French.

Monday _____

Tuesday _____

Wednesday _____

Thursday _____

Friday _____

Saturday _____

Sunday _____

What time is it? _____

It's noon. _____

It's midnight. _____

ANSWER KEY:
lundi (*Monday*); mardi (*Tuesday*); mercredi (*Wednesday*); jeudi (*Thursday*); vendredi (*Friday*); samedi (*Saturday*); dimanche (*Sunday*); Quelle heure est-il ? (*What time is it?*); Il est midi. (*It's noon.*); Il est minuit. (*It's midnight.*)

Grammar Builder 2
▶ 9E Grammar Builder 2 (CD 3, Track 8)

Notice that to answer the question quelle heure est-il ? (*what time is it?*) you just say:

il est (*it is*) + number + heure/heures (*hour/hours*)

So, il est cinq heures means *it's 5:00* (or literally, *it's five hours*).

(Note that you would write une heure for 1:00 but cinq heures for 5:00, since the phrases literally mean *one hour* and *five hours* respectively.)

Also:

... et demie	*half past ...*
... et quart	*a quarter past ...* or *a quarter after ...*

| ... moins le quart | a quarter to ... |

So:

Il est huit heures et demie.	It's half past eight.
Il est onze heures et quart.	It's a quarter past eleven./ It's a quarter after eleven.
Il est neuf heures moins le quart.	It's a quarter to nine.

It's important to note that most people in France use the 24-hour clock, so you'll see:

| Il est quinze heures. | It's 3:00 p.m. (literally, It's 15:00.) |
| Il est dix-huit heures. | It's 6:00 p.m. (literally, It's 18:00.) |

Take It Further

In addition to et demie, et quart, and moins le quart, you can also just say the appropriate number after heure/heures:

huit heures trente	8:30
deux heures trente-huit	2:38
onze heures cinq	11:05

Notice that, in French, you don't express the zero with minutes less than ten, as you do in English. In other words, you literally say *eleven five* in French instead of *eleven oh five* for 11:05.

It's important to mention that when you use the 24-hour clock after noon, you actually should **not** use the phrases et quart, et demie, or moins le quart. You should use numbers only. For example, you cannot say quatorze heures moins le quart (*a quarter to 2 p.m.*). Instead, you would have to say treize heures quarante-cinq (*1:45 p.m.*).

Not familiar with the 24-hour clock? It simply means that the hours in a day start at 0 and go up to 23. So:

0:00	12 a.m.
1:00	1 a.m.
2:00	2 a.m.
11:00	11 a.m.
12:00	12 p.m.
13:00	1 p.m.
14:00	2 p.m.
23:00	11 p.m.

There are no words for *a.m.* or *p.m.* in French; the 24-hour clock is used instead, or phrases like *in the morning* or *in the evening*. You'll learn more in the next Take It Further.

Also note that, in French, you will normally see the time written as shown on the left:

1h	1:00
8h30	8:30
15h45	15:45
0h15	0:15

The h, of course, stands for heure(s).

✎ Work Out 1

Okay, let's put everything you've learned so far together in a short comprehension exercise.

Below is a description of someone's day. Fill in the appropriate times in French. Make sure to write each time out in full.

▶ 9F Work Out 1 (CD 3, Track 9). Listen to the audio to practice pronouncing the sentences below! The audio also includes the French translations, so try to complete the exercise here first before listening.

Aujourd'hui c'est lundi, et la gérante va au travail.
It's Monday today, and the (female) manager goes to work.

Elle arrive à la gare à _____.
*She arrives at the train station at **8:10**.*

Elle prend le train à _____.
*She takes the train at **a quarter past eight**.*

Elle arrive au bureau à _____ **du matin.**
*She arrives at the office at **9:00** in the morning.*

Elle boit du café et lit ses emails. Elle parle avec ses collègues.
She drinks some coffee and reads her emails. She speaks with her colleagues.

Ils vont à une réunion à _____.
*They go to a meeting at **10:30**.*

Ils déjeunent ensemble à _____ .

*They have lunch together at **13:00 (1:00 p.m.)**.*

ANSWER KEY:

huit heures dix; huit heures et quart; neuf heures; dix heures trente (dix heures et demie); treize heures

---

Take It Further

Now you know how to tell time! Pretty easy, n'est-ce pas [nehs pah] (*isn't it*)?

Some new words you saw in the exercise include:

aujourd'hui	*today*
le matin	*the morning*
boire	*to drink*
l'email (*masc.*), le mail/mèl, le courriel, le courrier électronique	*the email*

Also, notice that the exercise used the phrase neuf heures du matin (*9:00 in the morning*). You know that France often uses the 24-hour clock, so why do you need to specify du matin (*in the morning*, or literally, *of the morning*) after neuf heures, since *9:00 p.m.* would be vingt et une heures (21:00)?

Well, the 24-hour clock isn't always used, especially in casual conversation, so you will often hear phrases like du matin, de l'après-midi (*in the afternoon*), and du soir (*in the evening, at night*) added after the time to clarify.

3 Use what you've learned to discuss professions and schedules

💬 Bring It All Together

Now let's bring it all together and add a little bit more vocabulary and structure. Read and listen to the following monologue and pay careful attention to how the times and days of the week are being used.

▶ 9G Bring It All Together (CD 3, Track 10)

The actress performs Sunday at 8:00.
L'actrice joue dimanche à huit heures.

The (male) teacher teaches on Mondays.
Le professeur enseigne le lundi.

The (male) singer sings Saturday at 10:00.
Le chanteur chante samedi à dix heures.

The (female) lawyer doesn't sing.
L'avocate ne chante pas.

The salesman never arrives before 9:00.
Le vendeur n'arrive jamais avant neuf heures.

The (female) director always works on the weekend.
La directrice travaille toujours le week-end.
Ⓘ

Take It Further

9H Take It Further (CD 3, Track 11)

You just saw a few examples of times and days being used in sentences. To say that something happens *at* a particular time, use the preposition à:

J'arrive à huit heures et demie.
I arrive at half past eight.

To say that something happens *on* a particular day, just say that day, as in:

Nous arrivons lundi.
We're arriving on Monday.

To say that something happens in general, use **le**:

Vous allez à l'école le lundi et le mercredi.
You go to school Mondays and Wednesdays.

Finally, don't forget that you can negate a verb by putting **ne** (**n'**) and **pas** around it:

je ne voyage pas	*I don't travel*
elle n'étudie pas	*she doesn't study*

If you use **jamais** instead of **pas** (in other words, if you use **ne... jamais**), that means *never*:

elle n'étudie jamais
she never studies

The opposite is toujours:

elle étudie toujours
she always studies

You also saw two new professions:

| le directeur/la directrice | the director, the manager (male/female) |
| le vendeur/la vendeuse | the salesman/the saleswoman |

Notice that the endings used in the two professions above (-eur/-rice, -eur/-euse) correspond with some of the endings you saw in Grammar Builder 1.

Finally, you also got a good chance to review the verb arriver (*to arrive, to get somewhere*), which you first saw at the end of Lesson 8.

✎ Work Out 2

▶ 9I Work Out 2 (CD 3, Track 12) for different, audio-only exercises!

Let's practice professions. Match each profession to the correct French translation.

1. *female doctor*	a. avocat
2. *male lawyer*	b. vendeur
3. *male teacher*	c. médecin
4. *actor*	d. professeur
5. *saleswoman*	e. cuisinier
6. *writer*	f. vendeuse
7. *male cook*	g. acteur
8. *salesman*	h. écrivain

ANSWER KEY:
1. c; 2. a; 3. d; 4. g; 5. f; 6. h; 7. e; 8. b

✎ Drive It Home

Now let's practice telling time. Fill in the blanks with heure or heures, and then read each sentence aloud.

1. Il est une _____ vingt. (*It's 1:20.*)

2. Il est trois _____ et quart. (*It's a quarter past three.*)

3. Il est vingt et une _____ quinze. (*It's 9:15 p.m.*)

4. Il est une _____ du matin. (*It's 1:00 in the morning.*)

5. Il est six _____ et demie du soir. (*It's half past six in the evening.*)

6. Il est vingt-trois _____ quarante. (*It's 11:40 p.m.*)

7. Il est quatorze _____ trente. (*It's 2:30 p.m.*)

8. Il est dix _____ cinquante-cinq. (*It's 10:55.*)

ANSWER KEY:
1 and 4 are heure and the rest are heures.

Parting Words

Félicitations !

You've finished the lesson! How did you do? You should now be able to:

☐ Talk about different professions (Still unsure? Go back to page 168)

☐ Say the days of the week (Still unsure? Go back to page 170)

☐ Tell time (Still unsure? Go back to page 171)

☐ Use what you've learned to discuss professions and schedules
(Still unsure? Go back to page 176)

Take It Further

9K Take It Further (CD 3, Track 14)

Now that you've learned *the days of the week*, or les jours de la semaine, you might want to know les mois de l'année (*the months of the year*). They're easy to understand:

MONTHS OF THE YEAR	
janvier	January
février	February
mars	March
avril	April
mai	May
juin	June
juillet	July
août	August
septembre	September
octobre	October
novembre	November
décembre	December

To say that something is *in* a particular month, say en (*in, to, into*), as in:

Mon anniversaire est en novembre.
My birthday is in November.

Seasons might come in handy, too:

au printemps*	in (the) spring
en été	in (the) summer
en automne	in (the) fall (in autumn)
en hiver	in (the) winter

* As you can see, you use en with all of the seasons except printemps, where you have to use au. Also note that all of the seasons are masculine nouns.

So you could say:

Il fait froid en hiver.	It's cold in winter.
Il fait chaud en été.	It's hot in summer.
Il pleut au printemps.	It rains in the spring.
Il fait du vent en automne.	It's windy in fall.
(or Il y a du vent en automne.)	

As you can see, the verb faire, which means *to do* and also *to make*, is often used in place of *to be* when talking about the weather in French:

Il fait froid.	It's cold.
Il fait chaud.	It's hot.
Il fait du vent.	It's windy.

Quel temps fait-il aujourd'hui ?

What is the weather today? (literally, What weather does it make today?)

Note that temps, pronounced [tah(m)], means both *weather* and *time*.

Don't forget to go to *www.livinglanguage.com/languagelab* to access your free online tools for this lesson: flashcards, games, and quizzes.

Word Recall

Now let's review vocabulary and grammar from previous lessons.

A. First, let's practice directions. Fill in the blanks with the phrases *Turn right.*, *Turn left.*, or *Go straight ahead.* in French.

1. _____

2. _____

3. _____

B. Now let's describe someone's day. Fill in the blanks with the correct il form of the following verbs:

rentrer	aller
se coucher	prendre
regarder	

1. Il _____ son petit déjeuner à six heures et demie.

   (He has his breakfast at half past six.)

2. Il _____ au travail à sept heures.

   (He goes to work at 7:00.)

3. Il _____ à six heures moins le quart.

   (He goes home at a quarter to six.)

4. Il _____ la télé à vingt heures.

   (He watches TV at 8 p.m.)

5. Il _____ à vingt-trois heures.

   (He goes to bed at 11 p.m.)

ANSWER KEY:
A: 1. Allez tout droit. 2. Tournez à gauche. 3. Tournez à droite.
B: 1. prend; 2. va; 3. rentre; 4. regarde; 5. se couche

Lesson 10: Socializing

Leçon dix : la vie sociale

In this lesson, we'll talk about all the things that you like to do for fun.
You'll learn how to:

1 Talk about entertainment activities and sports
Make a suggestion
Say whether you like or dislike something
Say when you *finish* something and what you *choose* to do

2 Talk about what you *want* and what you *can* do

3 Use what you've learned to talk about
likes, dislikes, and going out

Commençons ! *Let's begin!*

1 Talk about entertainment activities and sports
Make a suggestion
Say whether you like or dislike something
Say when you *finish* something and what you *choose* to do

Vocabulary Builder 1

(▷) 10B Vocabulary Builder 1 (CD 3, Track 16)

Let's go to the movies.	Allons au cinéma.
The film starts at 10 p.m. and finishes at midnight.	Le film commence à vingt-deux heures et finit à minuit.
Who's choosing the film?	Qui choisit le film ?
I have theatre tickets.	J'ai des places de théâtre.
We're going to a party tonight.	On va à une soirée ce soir.*
Let's go dance!	Allons danser !
I love this (night)club!	J'adore cette boîte (de nuit) !
We're having dinner at a friend's house.	Nous dînons chez un ami.
I like soccer.	J'aime le football.**
Do you like swimming?	Aimes-tu la natation ?
I prefer tennis.	Je préfère le tennis.
I don't like horseback riding.	Je n'aime pas l'équitation.

* Ce soir literally means *this evening* but it is also commonly used to mean *tonight*.

** Note that football (*soccer*) is often shortened to just foot in French, as you saw earlier in this course with stade de foot (*soccer stadium*).

Vocabulary Practice 1

Now let's practice what you just learned. As always, fill in the blanks with the correct French translations, and feel free to use a dictionary or the glossary if you need to.

Make sure to include the appropriate definite article (la, le, l') before each sport. If the definite article is l', remember to write down the gender as well.

(Hint: the French word for *ticket* is feminine.)

the film _____

a ticket _____

a party _____

this evening, tonight _____

a (night)club _____

soccer _____

swimming _____

tennis _____

horseback riding _____

ANSWER KEY:
le film (*the film*); une place (*a ticket*); une soirée (*a party*); ce soir (*this evening, tonight*); une boîte (de nuit) (*a [night]club*); le foot(ball) (*soccer*); la natation (*swimming*); le tennis (*tennis*); l'équitation (*f.*) (*horseback riding*)

Grammar Builder 1

▶ 10C Grammar Builder 1 (CD 3, Track 17)

There are a few things worth mentioning.

You can make a suggestion with the -ons form of a verb, so:

Allons... !	Let's go ... !
Sortons... !	Let's go out ... !

You also saw quite a few ways of expressing what you like or dislike:

j'aime	I like
je n'aime pas	I don't like

You can ask what someone else likes with:

aimes-tu... ?	do you like ... ?
est-ce que tu aimes... ?	do you like ... ?

Of course, you can be more polite by asking:

aimez-vous... ?	do you like ... ?
est-ce que vous aimez... ?	do you like ... ?

If you really *love* something, you can say j'adore, and je préfère means *I prefer*.

You also saw two examples of verbs that end in -ir in the infinitive: finir (*to finish*) and choisir (*to choose*). The conjugation of -ir verbs is a bit different from -er verbs. The singular forms *sound* the same (note the phonetics):

FINIR *(TO FINISH)* **AND** CHOISIR *(TO CHOOSE)*		
je finis	zhuh fee-nee	I finish
je choisis	zhuh shwah-zee	I choose
tu finis	tew fee-nee	you finish (familiar)
tu choisis	tew shwah-zee	you choose (familiar)
il ou elle finit	eel/ehl fee-nee	he or she finishes
il ou elle choisit	eel/ehl shwah-zee	he or she chooses

But in spelling, the je and tu forms end in -is, and the il/elle form ends in -it.

In the plural, these verbs take the same endings as -er verbs—that's -ons, -ez, and the silent -ent—but -iss is inserted first. So you have:

FINIR *(TO FINISH)* **AND** CHOISIR *(TO CHOOSE)*	
nous finissons	*we finish*
nous choisissons	*we choose*
vous finissez	*you finish (polite/plural)*
vous choisissez	*you choose (polite/plural)*
ils ou elles finissent	*they finish (masc. or fem.)*
ils ou elles choisissent	*they choose (masc. or fem.)*

Take It Further

You also saw two new -er verbs in Vocabulary Builder 1:

danser	*to dance*
dîner	*to dine, to have dinner*

And let's look at the infinitive forms of the verbs discussed in Grammar Builder 1:

sortir	*to go out, to leave*
aimer	*to like, to love*
adorer	*to love, to adore*
préférer	*to prefer*

Note that sortir is an irregular -ir verb, so it is not formed in the same way as finir and choisir. Fortunately, it's still pretty straightforward:

SORTIR (TO GO OUT, TO LEAVE)	
je sors	I go out
tu sors	you go out (familiar)
il sort	he goes out
elle sort	she goes out
nous sortons	we go out
vous sortez	you go out (polite/plural)
ils sortent	they go out (masc.)
elles sortent	they go out (fem.)

The verb partir (to leave, to go away) is conjugated in the same way.

Also, if you're going to talk about *going out, dining,* and *dancing,* then it's helpful to know the phrase en ville. You saw en ville used in Lesson 6 to mean *around town.* La ville means *the town* or *the city,* and en means *in/to/into,* so the phrase literally means *in/to/into town,* or *in/to/into the city,* but it can also be translated as *around town,* depending on the context.

Allons en ville !
Let's go into town!

Nous dînons en ville.
We're having dinner in the city.

Finally, you saw the new word chez in Vocabulary Builder 1. You'll learn more about chez later on in the lesson.

2 Talk about what you *want* and what you *can* do

Vocabulary Builder 2

▶ 10D Vocabulary Builder 2 (CD 3, Track 18)

I want ...	Je veux...
I want to go to the movies.	Je veux aller au cinéma.
Do you want to go to a party with me?	Veux-tu aller à une soirée avec moi ?
I like to go out to clubs. *(I like to go out clubbing.)*	J'aime sortir en boîte.
We want to go to the park.	Nous voulons aller au parc.
He wants to go to a (female) friend's house.	Il veut aller chez une amie.
The girls want to play soccer.	Les filles veulent jouer au foot.
I don't want to play tennis.	Je ne veux pas jouer au tennis.
We can go horseback riding. *(literally, We can do horseback riding.)*	Nous pouvons faire de l'équitation.
I can go swimming. *(literally, I can do swimming.)*	Je peux faire de la natation.
You can choose the restaurant.	Tu peux choisir le restaurant.

✎ Vocabulary Practice 2

Fill in the blanks with the correct French translations. Don't forget to use a dictionary or the glossary if you need to.

to go out to clubs, to go out clubbing _____

to go to the park _____

to play soccer _____

to play tennis _____

to go horseback riding _____

to go swimming _____

ANSWER KEY:

sortir en boîte (*to go out to clubs, to go out clubbing*); aller au parc (*to go to the park*); jouer au foot (*to play soccer*); jouer au tennis (*to play tennis*); faire de l'équitation (*to go horseback riding*); faire de la natation (*to go swimming*)

Grammar Builder 2

▶ 10E Grammar Builder 2 (CD 3, Track 19)

You've just seen some examples of the verbs vouloir (*to want*) and pouvoir (*can, to be able*). Both of these verbs can be used with another verb in the infinitive, so:

| je veux rester | I want to stay |
| je peux rester | I can stay (I am able to stay) |

These verbs are irregular, but a lot of the forms are pronounced in the same way (note the phonetics below). The conjugation of vouloir is:

VOULOIR (TO WANT)		
je veux	zhuh vuh	I want
tu veux	tew vuh	you want (familiar)
il veut	eel vuh	he wants
elle veut	ehl vuh	she wants
nous voulons	noo voo-loh(n)	we want
vous voulez	voo voo-lay	you want (polite/plural)
ils veulent	eel vuhl	they want (masc.)
elles veulent	ehl vuhl	they want (fem.)

The conjugation of pouvoir is:

POVOIR (CAN, TO BE ABLE TO)		
je peux	zhuh puh	I can
tu peux	tew puh	you can (familiar)
il peut	eel puh	he can
elle peut	ehl puh	she can
nous pouvons	noo poo-voh(n)	we can
vous pouvez	voo poo-vay	you can (polite/plural)
ils peuvent	eel puhv	they can (masc.)
elles peuvent	ehl puhv	they can (fem.)

Notice that you can also use the verbs aimer, adorer, and préférer with other infinitives, just like vouloir and pouvoir. So, you can say:

J'aime aller au cinéma.	I like to go to the movies.
J'adore aller au cinéma.	I love to go to the movies.
Je préfère aller au cinéma.	I prefer to go to the movies.
Je veux aller au cinéma.	I want to go to the movies.
Je peux aller au cinéma.	I can go to the movies. (I am able to go to the movies.)

Finally, notice that chez is used to mean at someone's house or place, so:

chez mes amis	at my friends' house
chez Marc	at Marc's house
chez moi	at my place (at home, at my home)

✎ Work Out 1

Let's practice! Try to translate the following paragraph using what you've learned so far. The only phrase you haven't seen yet is:

tous les + day of the week in the plural

For example: **tous les lundis** (*every Monday*), **tous les mercredis** (*every Wednesday*), etc.

▶ 10F Work Out 1 (CD 3, Track 20). Listen to the audio to practice pronouncing the following paragraph. The audio also includes the English translation, so try to translate the paragraph below first before listening.

Voici Camille. Camille est sportive. Elle aime jouer au tennis. Elle n'aime pas le cinéma. Jean préfère aller au théâtre. Jean va en ville tous les samedis. Jean va chez un ami. Ils adorent sortir en boîte.

_____

_____

_____

_____

⏸

ANSWER KEY:

Here is Camille. Camille is athletic. She likes to play tennis. She doesn't like the movies/movie theater. Jean prefers to go to the theater. Jean goes to town (into town, to/into the city) every Saturday. Jean goes to a (male) friend's house. They love to go out to clubs/to go out clubbing.

3 Use what you've learned to talk about likes, dislikes, and going out

◎ Bring It All Together

Now let's bring it all together and add a little bit more vocabulary and structure. Read and listen to the following dialogue between two new friends.

▶ 10G Bring It All Together (CD 3, Track 21)

A: *Hi, I'm Léon. I am athletic. And you?*
Salut, je suis Léon. Je suis sportif. Et toi ?

B: *No, I prefer the theater. I like movies and museums, too.*
Non, moi je préfère le théâtre. J'aime aussi le cinéma et les musées.

A: *Me too, I like museums!*
Moi aussi, j'aime les musées !

B: *Do you want to come with me?*
Veux-tu venir avec moi ?

A: *Okay.*
D'accord.

B: *After, there's a party at my friend's house. All my friends are coming.*
Après, il y a une fête chez mon ami. Tous mes amis viennent.

A: *Perfect. Let's go!*
Parfait. Allons-y !

⑪

Take It Further

▶ 10H Take It Further (CD 3, Track 22)

You saw one more common verb. That's the (irregular) verb **venir** (to come). The forms are:*

VENIR *(TO COME)*	
je viens	*I come*
tu viens	*you come (familiar)*
il vient	*he comes*
elle vient	*she comes*
nous venons	*we come*
vous venez	*you come (polite/plural)*
ils viennent	*they come (masc.)*
elles viennent	*they come (fem.)*
* Note that the verbs **revenir** *(to come back, to return)* and **devenir** *(to become)* are conjugated like **venir**.	

You can say, for example:

Je veux venir avec toi.
I want to come with you.

Notice that you use the pronoun **toi** (*you, familiar*) after **avec** (*with*). You could also say:

avec moi	*with me*
avec lui	*with him*
avec elle	*with her*

avec nous	with us
avec vous	with you (polite/plural)
avec eux	with them (masc.)
avec elles	with them (fem.)

These are good phrases to know when you're making plans:

| Tu veux venir au cinéma avec nous ce soir ? | Do you want to come to the movies with us tonight? |
| Non, je ne veux pas aller à la soirée avec eux. | No, I don't want to go to the party with them. |

Note that **moi, toi, lui**, etc. can also be used for emphasis, as in:

Non, moi je préfère le théâtre.
No, I prefer the theater.

This literally means *No, me I prefer the theater*, emphasizing that *I* prefer the theater, unlike *you*. Sometimes this type of emphasis is used in English as well, mainly in casual conversation: *You like playing sports, but me, I like the theater.*

You also saw the following new words:

la fête	the party, the festival, the holiday
parfait/parfaite	perfect
d'accord	okay, all right (literally, of agreement)

And remember that **tous les samedis** means *every Saturday* and **tous mes amis** means *all my friends*? Well, **tous** is actually the masculine plural form of **tout**, which means *all* or *every*. Here are all of the forms of **tout**:

masculine singular	**tout**
feminine singular	**toute**
masculine plural	**tous**
feminine plural	**toutes**

✎ Work Out 2

▶ 10| Work Out 2 (CD 3, Track 23) for different, audio-only exercises!

Let's do some basic practice of the important verb **venir**. Fill in the following table:

I come	
you come (familiar)	
he comes	
she comes	
we come	
you come (polite/plural)	
they come (masc.)	
they come (fem.)	

ANSWER KEY:
je viens; tu viens; il vient; elle vient; nous venons (on vient); vous venez; ils viennent; elles viennent

✎ Drive It Home

A. Let's practice making suggestions. Conjugate each verb in parentheses in the nous form.

1. _____ (aller) au cinéma !

   (Let's go to the movies/the movie theater!)

2. _____ (sortir) ce soir ! *(Let's go out tonight!)*

3. _____ (faire) de l'équitation ! *(Let's go horseback riding!)*

4. _____ (jouer) au tennis ! *(Let's play tennis!)*

5. _____ (regarder) le télé ! *(Let's watch television!)*

6. _____ (prendre) le métro ! *(Let's take the subway!)*

B. Now fill in the blanks with the correct form of the verb choisir *(to choose)*.

1. Je _____ le film. *(I choose the film.)*

2. Tu _____ le film. *(You choose the film.)*

3. Il _____ le film. *(He chooses the film.)*

4. Elle _____ le film. *(She chooses the film.)*

5. Nous _____ le film. *(We choose the film.)*

6. Vous _____ le film. *(You choose the film.)*

7. Ils _____ le film. *(They choose the film.)*

8. Elles _____ le film. *(They choose the film.)*

C. Fill in the blanks with the correct form of the verb vouloir (*to want*).

1. Je _____ sortir en boîte ce soir.

   (*I want to go out clubbing tonight.*)

2. _____-tu sortir en boîte ce soir ?

   (*Do you want to go out clubbing tonight?*)

3. Il _____ sortir en boîte ce soir.

   (*He wants to go out clubbing tonight.*)

4. Elle ne _____ pas sortir en boîte ce soir.

   (*She doesn't want to go out clubbing tonight.*)

5. Nous _____ sortir en boîte ce soir.

   (*We want to go out clubbing tonight.*)

6. _____-vous sortir en boîte ce soir ?

   (*Do you want to go out clubbing tonight?*)

7. Ils ne _____ pas sortir en boîte ce soir ?

   (*They don't want to go out clubbing tonight?*)

8. Est-ce qu'elles _____ sortir en boîte ce soir ?

   (*Do they want to go out clubbing tonight?*)

ANSWER KEY:
A: 1. Allons; 2. Sortons; 3. Faisons; 4. Jouons; 5. Regardons; 6. Prenons
B: 1. choisis; 2. choisis; 3. choisit; 4. choisit; 5. choisissons; 6. choisissez; 7. choisissent; 8. choisissent
C: 1. veux; 2. Veux; 3. veut; 4. veut; 5. voulons; 6. Voulez; 7. veulent; 8. veulent

Parting Words

You've learned the basic vocabulary you need to talk about some recreational activities. You should now be able to:

☐ Talk about entertainment activities and **les sports** *(masc.)* *(sports)* (Still unsure? Go back to page 185)

☐ Make a suggestion (Still unsure? Go back to page 186)

☐ Say whether you like or dislike something (Still unsure? Go back to page 187)

☐ Say when you *finish* something and what you *choose* to do (Still unsure? Go back to page 187)

☐ Talk about what you *want* and what you *can* do (Still unsure? Go back to page 191)

☐ Use what you've learned to talk about likes, dislikes, and going out (Still unsure? Go back to page 194)

Don't forget to go to *www.livinglanguage.com/languagelab* to access your free online tools for this lesson: flashcards, games, and quizzes.

Take It Further

10K Take It Further (CD 3, Track 25)

You may want to extend your vocabulary with some more popular activities:

le ski	skiing
l'alpinisme (masc.)	climbing
l'haltérophilie (fem.)	weight lifting
la course à pied	running
le patin à glace	ice skating
la voile	sailing
les jeux (masc.) électroniques	electronic games
la danse	dancing
la cuisine	cooking
la moto	motorcycling
prendre un verre avec des amis	having a drink with friends (to have a drink with friends)

À votre santé ! *To your health!*

And that brings us to the end of our last lesson! You can now test and practice what you've learned with the final Word Recall and self-graded quiz, followed by five conversational dialogues that will bring together the French you've seen so far.

Keep in mind that if you want to go back and review anything in the lessons at any time, you should always feel free to do so. Move at your own pace.

Bonne chance ! *Good luck!*

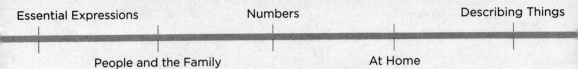

Word Recall

Now let's review vocabulary and grammar from previous lessons.

A. Remember how to tell time in French? Let's practice. Fill in the blanks below with the time indicated on each clock. Make sure to write each time out in full in French, and start with *It is ...* (but in French, of course!). Don't worry about the 24-hour clock.

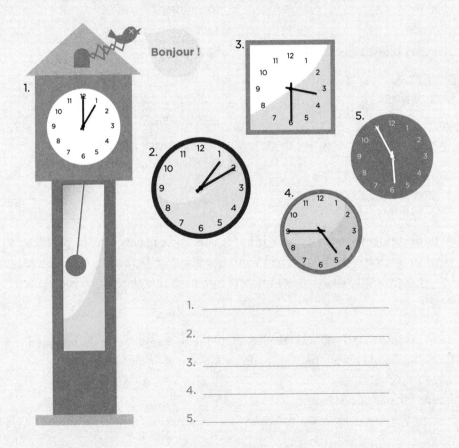

Bonjour !

1. _____

2. _____

3. _____

4. _____

5. _____

B. Now let's practice verbs. Match each French verb to its correct English translation:

1. commencer	a. *to want*
2. parler	b. *to show*
3. manger	c. *to start, to begin*
4. habiter	d. *to ask*
5. demander	e. *to understand*
6. vouloir	f. *to think*
7. donner	g. *to give*
8. écouter	h. *to sing*
9. penser	i. *to listen*
10. chanter	j. *to speak*
11. comprendre	k. *to live*
12. montrer	l. *to eat*

ANSWER KEY:
A: 1. Il est une heure. 2. Il est une heure dix. 3. Il est trois heures trente./Il est trois heures et demie. 4. Il est quatre heures quarante-cinq./Il est cinq heures moins le quart. 5. Il est cinq heures cinquante-cinq./Il est six heures moins cinq.
B: 1. c; 2. j; 3. l; 4. k; 5. d; 6. a; 7. g; 8. i; 9. f; 10. h; 11. e; 12. b

Quiz 2

Petit Test 2

You've completed all ten lessons! Bravo ! (*Well done!*)

Now let's review! In this section you'll find a final quiz testing what you learned in Lessons 1-10. Once you've completed it, score yourself to see how well you've done. If you find that you need to go back and review, please do so before continuing on to the Review Dialogues and comprehension questions.

A. Match the French expressions on the left to the correct English translations on the right.

1. **Ça va.**	a. *Good-bye.*
2. **Enchanté.**	b. *Hi.*
3. **Bonsoir.**	c. *Pleased to meet you.*
4. **Salut.**	d. *Good evening.*
5. **Au revoir.**	e. *I'm fine.*

B. Rewrite the following times using numbers instead of words. For example, you might write 0h30, 2h25, 18h12, etc.

1. Il est cinq heures quarante-sept. _____

2. Il est vingt-deux heures trente. _____

3. Il est minuit et quart. _____

4. Il est trois heures moins le quart. _____

5. Il est dix-huit heures cinquante-trois. _____

C. Fill in the blanks with the appropriate French adjective in the correct form.

1. Ce plat n'est pas bon ; ce plat est _____ .
   (This dish isn't good; it's bad.)

2. Ma maison est _____ ; il y a vingt-cinq pièces.
   (My house is big; there are 25 rooms.)

3. Mon grand-père a quatre-vingt-dix-huit ans. Il est _____ .
   (My grandfather is 98 years old. He is old.)

4. Elle fait de la natation et de l'équitation, et elle joue au tennis. Elle est

   _____ !

   (She goes swimming and horseback riding, and she plays tennis. She's athletic!)

5. Le drapeau américain est _____ , blanc et _____ .
   (The American flag is red, white, and blue.)

D. Conjugate the verbs in parentheses in the correct form and then translate each sentence into English.

1. Nous _____ (venir) à la soirée.

2. Vous _____ (fait) le ménage.

3. Ils _____ (prendre) le bus.

4. Elles _____ (aller) au restaurant.

5. Je _____ (pouvoir) aller à Paris.

E. Conjugate the following reflexive verbs in the correct form and then translate each sentence into English.

1. Vous _____ (s'appeler) Christine.

2. Elle _____ (se laver) à sept heures.

3. Je _____ (s'habiller) à huit heures.

4. Tu _____ (s'appeler) Jean.

5. Nous _____ (se coucher) à vingt-deux heures.

F. Rewrite the following sentences in the plural based on the English translations provided.

1. **Tu es américaine.** (*You are American.*)

   _____

   (*You [plural] are American.*)

2. **Cette chanteuse est petite !** (*That singer is short!*)

   _____

   (*Those singers are short!*)

3. **Ma nièce n'a pas son vélo.** (*My niece doesn't have her bike.*)

   _____

   (*My nieces don't have their bikes.*)

4. **Tu as une place de théâtre.** (*You have a theater ticket.*)

   _____

   (*You [plural] have theater tickets.*)

5. **La vieille femme a un livre.** (*The old woman has a book.*)

   _____

   (*The old women have a lot of books.*)

ANSWER KEY:

A: 1. e; 2. c; 3. d; 4. b; 5. a

B: 1. 5h47 2. 22h30 3. 0h15 4. 2h45 5. 18h53

C: 1. mauvais; 2. grande; 3. vieux; 4. sportive; 5. rouge, bleu

D: 1. venons (We come to the party.) 2. faites (You do the house cleaning.) 3. prennent (They take the bus.) 4. vont (They go to the restaurant.) 5. peux (I can go to Paris./I am able to go to Paris.)

E: 1. vous appelez (Your name is Christine./You are called Christine.) 2. se lave (She washes up/herself at 7:00.) 3. m'habille (I get dressed at 8:00.) 4. t'appelles (Your name is Jean./You are called Jean.) 5. nous couchons (We go to bed at 10 p.m.)

F: 1. Vous êtes américaines. 2. Ces chanteuses sont petites ! 3. Mes nièces n'ont pas leurs vélos. 4. Vous avez des places de théâtre. 5. Les vieilles femmes ont beaucoup de livres.

How Did You Do?

Give yourself a point for every correct answer, then use the following key to determine whether or not you're ready to move on:

0-11 points: It's probably best to go back and study the lessons again. Take as much time as you need to. Review the vocabulary lists and carefully read through each Grammar Builder section.

12-24 points: If the questions you missed were in sections A, B, or C, you may want to review the vocabulary again; if you missed answers mostly in sections D, E, or F, check the Grammar Builder sections to make sure you have your conjugations and other grammar basics down.

25-30 points: Feel free to move on to the Review Dialogues! Great job!

 **Points**

Review Dialogues
Bienvenue ! *Welcome!*

Here's your chance to practice everything you've mastered in ten lessons of *Living Language Essential French* with these five everyday dialogues. Each dialogue is followed by comprehension questions.

To practice your pronunciation, don't forget to listen to the audio! As always, look for ▶ and ⏸. You'll hear the dialogue in French first, then in French and English. Next, for practice, you'll do some role play by taking part in the conversation yourself!

Have fun!

Dialogue 1
TALKING ABOUT THE FAMILY

First, try to read (and listen to!) the whole dialogue in French. Then read and listen to the French and English together. How much did you understand? Next, take part in the role play exercise in the audio and answer the comprehension questions here in the book.

Note that there will be words and phrases in these dialogues that you haven't seen yet. This is because we want to give you the feel of a real French conversation. As a result, feel free to use your dictionary or the glossary if you're unclear about anything you see.

(▶) French Only – 12A Dialogue 1 French (CD 3, Track 27); French and English – 12B Dialogue 1 French and English (CD 3, Track 28); Role Play Exercise – 12C Dialogue 1 Exercise (CD 3, Track 29)

Corinne : J'ai une petite famille. Et toi, Jean-Louis ?

I have a small family. How about you, Jean-Louis?
(And you, Jean-Louis?)

Jean-Louis : Moi, j'ai une grande famille.

Me, I have a big family.

Corinne : Vous êtes combien ?

How many are you?

Jean-Louis : Il y a sept personnes dans ma famille.

There are seven people in my family. (not including Jean-Louis)

Corinne : Combien de frères as-tu ?

How many brothers do you have?

Jean-Louis : J'ai deux frères.

I have two brothers.

Corinne : Et combien de sœurs ?

And how many sisters?

Jean-Louis : J'ai trois sœurs. Avec moi, ça fait six enfants. Avec maman et papa, ça fait huit personnes en tout.

I have three sisters. With me, that's six children. With Mom and Dad, that's eight people in all.

Corinne : Oui, en effet, c'est une grande famille.

Yes, really, that is a big family.

Jean-Louis : Et dans ta famille, il y a combien de personnes ?

And in your family, how many people are there?

Corinne : Il y a quatre personnes : papa, maman, et moi. Je n'ai pas de frères ou de sœurs. Je suis fille unique.

There are four people: Dad, Mom, and me. I don't have any brothers or sisters. I'm an only child.

Jean-Louis :	Mais qui est la quatrième personne ?
	But who's the fourth person?
Corinne :	C'est ma grand-mère. Elle habite chez nous.
	That's my grandmother. She lives with us. (She lives at our house.)
Jean-Louis :	Que fait ton père ?
	What does your father do?
Corinne :	Il est musicien. Et ton père ?
	He's a musician. And your father?
Jean-Louis :	Mon père et ma mère sont profs.
	My father and my mother are professors.
Corinne :	Ma mère est prof aussi, à l'université.
	My mother is also a professor, at the university.
Jean-Louis :	Quelle coïncidence !
	What a coincidence!

Dialogue 1 Practice

Now let's check your comprehension of the dialogue and review what you learned in Lessons 1-10 with the following exercises. Ready?

A. You saw a few new words for members of the family in the dialogue. What are they?

1. _____ *(Mom)*

2. _____ *(Dad)*

3. _____ *(only child, female)*

And now let's review the other family vocabulary you saw. Don't forget to translate the definite articles!

4. _____ (the mother)

5. _____ (the father)

6. _____ (the brother)

7. _____ (the sister)

8. _____ (the children)

9. _____ (the grandmother)

10. _____ (the family)

B. In the dialogue, you saw the phrase avec moi (*with me*). Rewrite that phrase to match each of the English phrases below.

1. *with you (familiar)* _____

2. *with her* _____

3. *with them (masc.)* _____

4. *with us* _____

5. *with him* _____

C. You also saw a few new question words in the dialogue. Fill in the table below with the new question words:

how many	1.
what	2.

Now let's review the question words you learned earlier in the course. Fill in the table below with the correct French translations. If the question word has a masculine and feminine form, make sure to include both of them.

where	3.
which, what	4.
how	5.
who	6.
what	7.

ANSWER KEY:

A: 1. maman; 2. papa; 3. fille unique; 4. la mère; 5. le père; 6. le frère; 7. la sœur; 8. les enfants; 9. la grand-mère; 10. la famille

B: 1. avec toi; 2. avec elle; 3. avec eux; 4. avec nous; 5. avec lui

C: 1. combien (de); 2. que; 3. où; 4. quel/quelle; 5. comment; 6. qui; 7. qu'est-ce que

Dialogue 2
THE NEW HOUSE

As with Dialogue 1, first read and listen to the whole dialogue in French. Then read and listen to the French and English together. How much did you understand? Next, do the role play in the audio as well as the comprehension exercises here in the book.

French Only – 13A Dialogue 2 French (CD 3, Track 30); French and English – 13B Dialogue 2 French and English (CD 3, Track 31); Role Play Exercise – 13C Dialogue 2 Exercise (CD 3, Track 32)

Thierry : Salut, Naomi, bienvenue dans ma nouvelle maison !
Hi, Naomi, welcome (in)to my new house!

Naomi : Combien de pièces y a-t-il ?
How many rooms are there?

Thierry :   Il y a neuf pièces. Veux-tu faire un tour de la maison ?

There are nine rooms. Do you want to take a tour of the house?

Naomi :   Avec plaisir.

With pleasure.

Thierry :   Voilà le salon, avec un canapé confortable, une vieille pendule
et une grande télé.

*Here's the living room, with a comfortable sofa, an old (grandfather)
clock, and a large TV.*

Naomi :   Et ensuite...

And then ...

Thierry :   Maintenant nous entrons dans la salle à manger, avec sa belle
table et son lustre.

*Now we enter (into) the dining room, with its beautiful table and its
chandelier.*

Naomi :   C'est très joli. Et où est la cuisine ?

It's very nice. And where is the kitchen?

Thierry :   La cuisine ? C'est tout droit. Entrons. Il y a un grand
réfrigérateur et un micro-ondes.

*The kitchen? It's straight ahead. Let's go in. (literally, Let's enter.)
There is a large refrigerator and a microwave (oven).*

Naomi :   Et par ici, qu'est-ce que c'est ?

And what is this way? (literally, And this way, what is this?)

Thierry :   Voici la bibliothèque, ma pièce préférée. Il y a beaucoup de
beaux livres, non ?

*Here's the library, my favorite room. There are a lot of beautiful
books, no?*

Naomi :   Oui. Quelle collection !

Yes. What a collection!

Thierry :   Et maintenant, voyons les chambres. Il y en a trois.

And now, let's see the bedrooms. There are three of them.

Naomi :   Chaque enfant a sa propre chambre ?

Each child has his or her own bedroom?

Thierry :	Oui, et ils ont chacun un ordinateur !
	Yes, and they each have a computer!
Naomi :	Thierry, où sont les toilettes ?
	Thierry, where is the toilet?
Thierry :	À côté de ma chambre. Et la salle de bains aussi.
	*Next to my bedroom. And the bathroom, too.**
Naomi :	Merci. Tu m'excuses un moment ?
	Thank you. Will you excuse me a moment?
Thierry :	Bien sûr.
	Of course.

* Note that, in France, the toilet and the bathroom (where you shower/take a bath and wash your hands) are typically separate rooms.

✎ Dialogue 2 Practice

In that dialogue, you saw a lot of vocabulary—both familiar and new—relating to rooms and objects in a house.

A. First, let's review the rooms in a house. Match the following French words to the correct English translations.

1. *the room*	a. la chambre (à coucher)
2. *the toilet*	b. la pièce
3. *the living room*	c. la salle à manger
4. *the kitchen*	d. la bibliothèque
5. *the bedroom*	e. la salle de bains
6. *the dining room*	f. les toilettes (fem.)
7. *the library*	g. la cuisine
8. *the bathroom*	h. le salon

B. Now let's review the objects in a house. Match the following French words to the correct English translations.

1. *the sofa*	a. le micro-ondes
2. *the chandelier*	b. la pendule
3. *the computer*	c. le canapé
4. *the microwave (oven)*	d. la télé
5. *the TV*	e. la table
6. *the refrigerator*	f. le lustre
7. *the grandfather clock*	g. le réfrigérateur
8. *the table*	h. l'ordinateur (masc.)
9. *the book*	i. le livre

ANSWER KEY:
A: 1. b; 2. f; 3. h; 4. g; 5. a; 6. c; 7. d; 8. e
B: 1. c; 2. f; 3. h; 4. a; 5. d; 6. g; 7. b; 8. e; 9. i

◖ Dialogue 3
GETTING AROUND TOWN

Remember, feel free to use your dictionary or the glossary to look up any words you don't know.

▶ French Only – 14A Dialogue 3 French (CD 3, Track 33); French and English – 14B Dialogue 3 French and English (CD 3, Track 34); Role Play Exercise – 14C Dialogue 3 Exercise (CD 3, Track 35)

Colette :	**Vous êtes perdu ?**
	Are you lost?

Omar : Oui, mademoiselle. Où est la pharmacie, s'il vous plaît ?
Yes, miss. Where's the drugstore, please?

Colette : La pharmacie ? Il faut traverser le pont.
The drugstore? You have to cross the bridge.

Omar : C'est près d'ici ?
Is it near here?

Colette : Non, c'est assez loin. Après le pont, il faut prendre la première rue à droite et descendre jusqu'au boulevard...
No, it's quite far. After the bridge, you have to take the first street on the right and go down until the boulevard ...

Omar : Oui, et au boulevard ?
Yes, and at the boulevard?

Colette : Vous traversez le boulevard et vous montez jusqu'au parc.
You cross the boulevard and you go up to the park.

Omar : C'est tout ?
Is that all?

Colette : Non, vous traversez le parc et vous arrivez devant une grande statue...
No, you cross the park and you arrive in front of a big statue ...

Omar : Une grande statue, oui... Et puis ?
A big statue, yes ... And then?

Colette : Vous passez à gauche de la statue, et la pharmacie est dans la quatrième rue à gauche.
You go (pass) to the left of the statue, and the drugstore is on (literally, in) the fourth street to the left.

Omar : Ah, enfin ! C'est bien compliqué. Merci, mademoiselle.
Oh, finally! It sure is complicated. Thank you, miss.

Colette : Je vous en prie, monsieur.
You're welcome, sir.

Omar : Mais j'ai aussi une lettre à mettre à la poste. Où est la poste, s'il vous plaît ?
But I also have a letter to mail. Where's the post office, please?

Colette :	La poste ? C'est tout près d'ici.
	The post office? It's very close to here.
Omar :	Super ! Dans quelle direction ?
	Great! In which direction?
Colette :	Vous allez tout droit. Elle est devant vous.
	You go straight ahead. It's in front of you.
Omar :	Alors, ça, c'est moins compliqué !
	Now, that's less complicated! (literally, Well, that, that's less complicated!)

✎ Dialogue 3 Practice

You saw a variety of verbs in that dialogue, so for this practice section, let's review verbs.

A. Each phrase below is from the dialogue and contains one verb. Identify the verb and then write its infinitive form in the blank space provided, followed by the English translation. (There may be several English translations for a verb; just write down one.)

For example, if the phrase was il fait froid, you would write down faire (*to do*).

1. vous êtes perdu _____

2. où est la pharmacie _____

3. prendre la première rue à droite _____

4. vous traversez le parc _____

5. vous arrivez devant une grande statue _____

6. j'ai aussi une lettre _____

7. vous allez tout droit_____

B. Now conjugate each of those infinitives in the tu form. For example, if the verb was faire, you would write tu fais.

1. _____

2. _____

3. _____

4. _____

5. _____

6. _____

7. _____

ANSWER KEY:

A: 1. être (to be); 2. être (to be); 3. prendre (to take); 4. traverser (to cross, to go across); 5. arriver (to arrive, to get somewhere, to reach); 6. avoir (to have); 7. aller (to go)

B: 1. tu es; 2. tu es; 3. tu prends; 4. tu traverses; 5. tu arrives; 6. tu as; 7. tu vas

◖ Dialogue 4

AT A RESTAURANT

How are you doing so far? Ready to try another dialogue? (Hint: le serveur means the waiter.)

▶ French Only – 15A Dialogue 4 French (CD 3, Track 36); French and English – 15B Dialogue 4 French and English (CD 3, Track 37); Role Play Exercise – 15C Dialogue 4 Exercise (CD 3, Track 38)

Élodie : **Monsieur, apportez-moi le menu, s'il vous plaît.**
Sir, bring me the menu, please.

Le serveur : **Voilà, madame.**
Here it is, madam.

Élodie : **Quelle est la soupe du jour ?**
What's the soup of the day?

Le serveur : **C'est la bisque de homard, madame.**
It's lobster bisque, madam.

Élodie : **Et quels sont les hors-d'œuvre ?**
And what are the appetizers?

Le serveur : **Nous avons des crudités ou du pâté maison.**
We have crudités or homemade pâté.

Élodie : **Hmm, vous avez aussi de la soupe à l'oignon ?**
Hmm, do you also have onion soup?

Le serveur : **Oui, madame, et elle est excellente !**
Yes, madam, and it is excellent!

Élodie : **Alors, donnez-moi une soupe à l'oignon.**
Then, give me an onion soup.

Le serveur : **Et comme plat principal, madame ?**
And as a main dish, madam?

Élodie : **Donnez-moi une côte de bœuf avec des pommes de terre.**
Give me a beef rib (bone-in ribeye) with potatoes.

Le serveur : **Et comme boisson ?**
And as a drink?

Élodie : **Du vin rouge, s'il vous plaît.**
Some red wine, please.

Le serveur : **Et pour le dessert, madame ?**
And for dessert, madam?

Élodie : **Une mousse au chocolat et un café-crème.**
A chocolate mousse and a coffee with cream.

Le serveur :   Voilà.
                Here it is.
Élodie :   Merci, monsieur. Apportez-moi l'addition, s'il vous plaît.
                Thank you, sir. Bring me the check, please.

⏸

✎ Dialogue 4 Practice

A. Vrai (*true*) or faux (*false*)? Next to each sentence, write down V for vrai or F for faux.

1. **Les hors-d'œuvre : Élodie choisit les crudités.** _____

2. **Le plat principal : Élodie mange de la viande.** _____

3. **La boisson : Élodie veut du vin.** _____

4. **Le dessert : Élodie n'aime pas le dessert.** _____

B. Below are some of the vocabulary words you saw in the dialogue. Next to each one, write un or une and then translate the phrase into English.

1. _____ soupe _____

2. _____ addition _____

3. _____ pomme de terre _____

4. _____ plat _____

5. _____ café-crème _____

6. _____ mousse au chocolate _____

7. _____ menu _____

8. _____ côte de bœuf _____

ANSWER KEY:

A: 1. F (No, she chooses onion soup, not crudités, as an appetizer); 2. V (Yes, she is eating meat for her main course); 3. V (Yes, she does want wine as her drink); 4. F (No, she does like dessert; she has a chocolate mousse and coffee with cream for dessert)

B: 1. une soupe (*one/a soup*); 2. une addition (*one/a check*); 3. une pomme de terre (*one/a potato*); 4. un plat (*one/a dish*); 5. un café-crème (*one/a coffee with cream*); 6. une mousse au chocolat (*one/a chocolate mousse*); 7. un menu (*one/a menu*); 8. une côte de bœuf (*one/a beef rib, one/a bone-in ribeye*)

◀ Dialogue 5
GOING TO THE MOVIES

Last one! You're almost done with *Essential French*, so let's talk about something fun: the movies. Enjoy!

▶ French Only – 16A Dialogue 5 French (CD 3, Track 39); French and English – 16B Dialogue 5 French and English (CD 3, Track 40); Role Play Exercise – 16C Dialogue 5 Exercise (CD 3, Track 41)

Joël :	Allô, Liliane ?
	Hello, Liliane?
Liliane :	Oui, qui est à l'appareil ?
	Yes, who is calling?
Joël :	C'est Joël. Veux-tu venir au cinéma avec moi samedi soir ?
	It's Joël. Do you want to come to the movies with me Saturday night?
Liliane :	Oui, d'accord. Qu'est-ce qu'on donne ?
	Yes, okay. What are they showing?
Joël :	Le dernier film de Hugh Grant.
	Hugh Grant's last (latest) film.
Liliane :	Est-ce que c'est en version originale* ?
	Is it in the original version?

Joël :	Oui, bien sûr, et il y a des sous-titres.
	Yes, of course, and there are subtitles.
Liliane :	Parfait. Je n'aime pas les films doublés.
	Perfect. I don't like dubbed movies.
Joël :	J'aime les comédies romantiques.
	I like romantic comedies.
Liliane :	Moi aussi. Et j'aime beaucoup Hugh Grant.
	Me too. And I like Hugh Grant a lot.
Joël :	J'aime aussi les films d'action et les films policiers.
	I also like action films and crime dramas.
Liliane :	Moi, je n'aime pas les films policiers.
	Me, I don't like crime dramas.
Joël :	Même pas avec Robert de Niro ?
	Not even with Robert de Niro?
Liliane :	Ah, si Robert de Niro joue dans le film, c'est différent. Et ce week-end, on va dîner ensemble avant le film ?
	Oh, if Robert de Niro is acting in the film, that's different. And this weekend, we'll have dinner together before the film?
Joël :	Oui. Il y a un nouveau restaurant vietnamien dans le coin.
	Yes. There's a new Vietnamese restaurant in the neighborhood.
Liliane :	Super. J'adore la nourriture vietnamienne.
	Super. I love Vietnamese food.

* In French, la version originale (*original version*)—commonly abbreviated v.o.—of a movie means that the film is in its original language and hasn't been dubbed into French (although it usually has French subtitles). On the other hand, v.f. (or la version française) means that the movie has been dubbed into French.

✎ Dialogue 5 Practice

A. Let's review adjectives, starting with the ones you saw in the dialogue. Fill in the table below with the masculine and feminine singular form of each adjective. If the adjective has two different masculine forms, make sure to include both of them.

MASCULINE SINGULAR	FEMININE SINGULAR	ENGLISH
1.		original
2.		new
3.		Vietnamese

Now let's review some of the other adjectives that you know. Fill in the table below.

MASCULINE SINGULAR	FEMININE SINGULAR	ENGLISH
4.		beautiful, handsome
5.		old
6.		happy
7.		dear, expensive

B. Translate the following phrases into English.

1. la comédie romantique _____

2. le film doublé _____

3. le film d'action _____

4. le film policier _____

5. les sous-titres _____

ANSWER KEY:

A: 1. original, originale; 2. nouveau/nouvel, nouvelle; 3. vietnamien, vietnamienne; 4. beau/bel, belle; 5. vieux/vieil, vieille; 6. heureux, heureuse; 7. cher, chère

B: 1. *the romantic comedy*; 2. *the dubbed movie/film*; 3. *the action movie/film*; 4. *the crime drama*; 5. *the subtitles*

You've come to the end of *Living Language Essential French*! Congratulations! We hope you've enjoyed your experience. If you bought *Complete French*, you can now continue on to *Intermediate French*. And of course, feel free to go back and review at any time if you need to.

For more information on other Living Language French courses and supplementary materials, visit www.livinglanguage.com.

Pronunciation Guide

Consonants

Note that the letter h can act as either a vowel or a consonant. See the end of the Pronunciation Guide for more information.

FRENCH	APPROXIMATE SOUND	PHONETIC SYMBOL	EXAMPLES
b, d, f, k, m, n, p, t, v, z	same as in English	same as in English	
ç	*s*	[s]	français [frah(n)-seh] (*French*)
c before a, o, u	*k*	[k]	cave [kahv] (*cellar*)
c before e, i, y	*s*	[s]	cinéma [see-nay-mah] (*movie theater*)
ch	*sh* sometimes *k*	[sh], [k]	chaud [shoh] (*hot*) psychologie [psee-koh-loh-zhee] (*psychology*)
g before a, o, u	*g* in *game*	[g]	gâteau [gah-toh] (*cake*)
g before e, i, y	*s* in *measure*	[zh]	âge [ahzh] (*age*)
gn	*ni* in *onion*	[ny]	agneau [ah-nyoh] (*lamb*)
j	*s* in *measure*	[zh]	jeu [zhuh] (*game*)
l	*l*	[l]	lent [lah(n)] (*slow*)
l when it's at the end of the word and follows i	*y* in *yes*	[y]	fauteuil [foh-tuhy] (*armchair*)
ll	*ll* in *ill*	[l]	elle [ehl] (*she*)

FRENCH	APPROXIMATE SOUND	PHONETIC SYMBOL	EXAMPLES
ll between i and e	y in yes	[y]	fille [feey] (girl, daughter)
qu, final q	k	[k]	qui [kee] (who), cinq [sa(n)k] (five)
r	pronounced in the back of the mouth, like a light gargling sound	[r]	Paris [pah-ree] (Paris)
s between vowels	z in zebra	[z]	maison [meh-zoh(n)] (house)
s at the beginning of a word or before/after a consonant	s	[s]	salle [sahl] (hall, room), course [koors] (errand)
ss	s	[s]	tasse [tahs] (cup)
th	t	[t]	thé [tay] (tea)
w	v	[v]	wagon-lit [vah-goh(n)-lee] (sleeping car)
x usually before a vowel	x in exact	[gz]	exact [ehg-zahkt] (exact)
x before a consonant or final e	x in exterior	[ks]	extérieur [ehks-tay-ree-uhr] (outside)

Keep in mind that most final consonants are silent in French, as with the -s in Paris [pah-ree] (Paris). However, there are five letters that are often (but not always) pronounced when final: c, f, l, q, and r.

French speakers also pronounce some final consonants when the next word begins with a vowel or silent h (see the end of the Pronunciation Guide for more information on the "silent h"). This is known as liaison [lyeh-zoh(n)] (*link*).

For example, the -s in nous [noo] (*we*) normally isn't pronounced. However, if it's followed by a word that begins with a vowel, such as allons [ah-loh(n)], then you do pronounce it: nous allons [noo zah-loh(n)] (*we go*). Notice that, in liaison, the s is pronounced *z* and it is "linked" to the following word: [zah-loh(n)].

Here's another example of liaison: un grand arbre [uh(n) grah(n) tahr-bruh] (*a big tree*). Normally, the -d in grand [grah(n)] is not pronounced, but, in liaison, it is pronounced *t* and linked to the following word.

Vowels

FRENCH	APPROXIMATE SOUND	PHONETIC SYMBOL	EXAMPLES
a, à, â	*a* in *father*	[ah]	laver [lah-vay] (*to wash*), à [ah] (*in, to, at*)
é, er, ez (end of a word), et	*ay* in *lay*	[ay]	été [ay-tay] (*summer*), aller [ah-lay] (*to go*), ballet [bah-lay] (*ballet*)
è, ê, ei, ai, aî	*e* in *bed*, with relaxed lips	[eh]	père [pehr] (*father*), forêt [foh-reh] (*forest*), faire [fehr] (*to do*)

FRENCH	APPROXIMATE SOUND	PHONETIC SYMBOL	EXAMPLES
e without an accent (and not combined with another vowel or r, z, t)	*a* in *above,* or *e* in *bed* with relaxed lips, or silent	[uh] or [eh] or n/a	le [luh] (*the*), belle [behl] (*beautiful*), danse [dah(n)s] (*dance*)
eu, œu followed by a consonant sound	*u* in *fur* with lips very rounded and loose	[uh]	cœur [kuhr] (*heart*)
eu, œu not followed by any sound	*u* in *fur* with lips very rounded and tight	[uh]	feu [fuh] (*fire*)
eille, ey	*ey* in *hey*	[ehy]	bouteille [boo-tehy] (*bottle*)
euille, œil	*a* in *above* + *y* in *yesterday*	[uhy]	œil [uhy] (*eye*)
i	*ee* in *beet*	[ee]	ici [ee-see] (*here*)
i plus vowel	*ee* in *beet* + *y* in *yesterday*	[y]	violon [vyoh-loh(n)] (*violin*)
o, au, eau, ô	*o* in *both*	[oh]	mot [moh] (*word*), eau [oh] (*water*), hôtel [oh-tehl] (*hotel*)
oi	*wa* in *watt*	[wah]	moi [mwah] (*me*)
ou	*oo* in *boot*	[oo]	vous [voo] (*you*)
ou before a vowel	*w* in *week*	[w]	ouest [wehst] (*west*), oui [wee] (*yes*)
oy	*wa* in *watt* + *y* in *yesterday*	[wah-y]	foyer [fwah-yay] (*home*)

FRENCH	APPROXIMATE SOUND	PHONETIC SYMBOL	EXAMPLES
u	keep your lips rounded as you pronounce *ee* in *beet*	[ew]	tu [tew] (*you*)
ui	*wee* in *week*	[wee]	lui [lwee] (*he, him, her*)

Nasal Vowels

FRENCH	APPROXIMATE SOUND	PHONETIC SYMBOL	EXAMPLES
an/en or am/em	*a* in *balm,* pronounced through both the mouth and the nose	[ah(n)] or [ah(m)]	France [frah(n)s] (*France*), entrer [ah(n)-tray] (*to enter*), emmener [ah(m)-muh-nay] (*to take along*)
in/yn/ain/ein or im/ym/aim/eim	*a* in *mad,* pronounced through both the mouth and the nose	[a(n)] or [a(m)]	vin [va(n)] (*wine*), vain [va(n)] (*vain*), sympa [sa(m)-pah] (*cool, nice, good*), faim [fa(m)] (*hunger*)
ien	*ee* in *beet* + *y* in *yesterday* + nasal *a* in *mad*	[ya(n)]	rien [rya(n)] (*nothing*)
oin	*w* + nasal *a* in *mad*	[wa(n)]	loin [lwa(n)] (*far*)

FRENCH	APPROXIMATE SOUND	PHONETIC SYMBOL	EXAMPLES
on or om	*o* in *song,* pronounced through both the mouth and the nose	[oh(n)] or [oh(m)]	bon [boh(n)] (*good*), tomber [toh(m)-bay] (*to fall*)
ion	*ee* in *beet* + *y* in *yesterday* + nasal *o* in *song*	[yoh(n)]	station [stah-syoh(n)] (*station*)
un or um	*u* in *lung,* pronounced through both the mouth and the nose	[uh(n)] or [uh(m)]	un [uh(n)] (*one, a/an*), parfum [pahr-fuh(m)] (*perfume*)

The Letter H

In French, the letter h is not pronounced. For example, huit (*eight*) would be pronounced [weet].

However, there are actually two different types of h in French: the silent or mute h and the aspirated h. While you wouldn't pronounce either one, they behave differently.

The silent h acts like a vowel. For example, words like le, la, se, de, and so on become "contracted" (l', s', d', etc.) before a silent h:

l'homme (le + homme)	*the man*
s'habiller (se + habiller)	*to get dressed*

Also, you usually use liaison with a silent h. For instance, les hommes would be pronounced [lay zohm].

However, the aspirated h acts like a consonant. Words like le, la, se, de, etc. do **not** become l', s', d', and so on before an aspirated h:

le homard	the lobster
se hâter	to rush

Also, you do not use liaison with an aspirated h: les homards would be pronounced [lay oh-mahr].

Most h are silent, not aspirated. Still, there are many words that begin with an aspirated h. Unfortunately, there isn't an easy way to tell which are which. Just start by learning the common ones, and then continue memorizing others that you come across.

Apart from homme and habiller, here are some other examples of common words that begin with a silent h: habiter (*to live*), heure (*hour*), heureux/heureuse (*happy*), hier (*yesterday*), hôpital (*hospital*), horaire (*schedule*), and huile (*oil*). Apart from homard and hâter, here are some other examples of common words that begin with an aspirated h: huit (*eight*), héros (*hero*), haine (*hatred*), hasard (*chance*), hâte (*haste*), haut (*high*), honte (*shame*), and hors (*outside*).

Grammar Summary

Here is a brief snapshot of French grammar from this course. Keep in mind that there are exceptions to many grammar rules.

1. NUMBERS

CARDINAL		ORDINAL	
un/une	one	premier/première	first
deux	two	deuxième, second/seconde	second
trois	three	troisième	third
quatre	four	quatrième	fourth
cinq	five	cinquième	fifth
six	six	sixième	sixth
sept	seven	septième	seventh
huit	eight	huitième	eighth
neuf	nine	neuvième	ninth
dix	ten	dixième	tenth

2. ARTICLES

	DEFINITE		INDEFINITE	
	Singular	Plural	Singular	Plural
Masculine	le	les	un	des
Feminine	la	les	une	des

Note that l' is used instead of le and la before words beginning with a vowel or silent h.

3. CONTRACTIONS

de + le = du (*some/of the, masculine*)

de + les = des (*some/of the, plural*)

à + le = au (*to/at/in the, masculine*)

à + les = aux (*to/at/in the, plural*)

There is no contraction with la or l'.

4. PLURALS

Most nouns add -s to form the plural. However, nouns ending in -eau or -eu, and some nouns ending in -ou, add -x instead of -s to form the plural.

5. ADJECTIVES

Adjectives agree with the nouns they modify in gender and number; that is, they are masculine if the noun is masculine, plural if the noun is plural, etc.

a. The feminine of an adjective is normally formed by adding -e to the masculine singular.

b. If the masculine singular already ends in -e, the adjective has the same form in the feminine.

c. Some adjectives double the final consonant of the masculine singular form and then add -e to form the feminine.

d. The plural of adjectives is usually formed by adding -s to the masculine or feminine singular form.

6. POSSESSIVE ADJECTIVES

Possessive adjectives agree in gender and number with the possession.

BEFORE SINGULAR NOUNS		BEFORE PLURAL NOUNS	
Masculine	Feminine	Masculine and Feminine	
mon	ma	mes	*my*
ton	ta	tes	*your (familiar)*
son	sa	ses	*his, her, its*
notre	notre	nos	*our*
votre	votre	vos	*your (polite/plural)*
leur	leur	leurs	*their*

Before feminine singular nouns beginning with a vowel or silent h, use mon, ton, and son.

7. PRONOUNS

	SUBJECT	STRESSED	REFLEXIVE
1st singular	je/j'	moi	me/m'
2nd singular	tu	toi	te/t'
3rd masculine singular	il	lui	se/s'
3rd feminine singular	elle	elle	se/s'
1st plural	nous	nous	nous
2nd plural	vous	vous	vous
3rd masculine plural	ils	eux	se / s'
3rd feminine plural	elles	elles	se / s'

On is an indefinite subject pronoun that means *we, one,* or *people/you/they in general.*

Stressed pronouns are generally used after prepositions (**avec moi**, etc.) or for emphasis (**moi, j'ai vingt ans**).

8. QUESTION WORDS

où	*where*
qu'est-ce que	*what*
quel/quelle, quels/quelles	*which, what*
qui	*who*
comment	*how*

9. DEMONSTRATIVE ADJECTIVES

Masculine Singular	ce	*this, that*
Masculine Singular (before a vowel or silent **h**)	cet	*this, that*
Feminine Singular	cette	*this, that*
Masculine Plural	ces	*these, those*
Feminine Plural	ces	*these, those*

When it is necessary to distinguish between *this* and *that*, **-ci** and **-là** are added to the noun: **Donnez-moi ce livre-ci.** (*Give me this book.*)

10. NEGATION

A sentence is made negative by placing ne before the verb and pas after it. When placed before a vowel or silent h, ne becomes n'.

11. VERBS

There are three types of French verbs:

TYPE	EXAMPLE
verbs ending in -er	parler (*to speak*)
verbs ending in -ir	finir (*to finish*)
verbs ending in -re	vendre (*to sell*)

For regular verbs, the present tense is formed by taking the -er, -ir, or -re off the infinitive and adding the following endings:

PRONOUN	-ER VERB ENDING	-IR VERB ENDING	-RE VERB ENDING
je	-e	-is	-s
tu	-es	-is	-s
il/elle*	-e	-it	- (no ending added)
nous	-ons	-issons	-ons
vous	-ez	-issez	-ez
ils/elles	-ent	-issent	-ent

* Remember that on (*we, one, people in general*) has the same verb form as il and elle.

The verbs aller (*to go*), venir (*to come*), and prendre (*to take*) are examples of irregular verbs. Although they end in -er, -ir, and -re respectively, they are not formed as shown above.

12. ÊTRE AND AVOIR

ÊTRE (TO BE)	
je suis	I am
tu es	you are (familiar)
il est	he is
elle est	she is
nous sommes	we are
vous êtes	you are (polite/plural)
ils sont	they are (masculine)
elles sont	they are (feminine)

AVOIR (TO HAVE)	
j'ai	I have
tu as	you have (familiar)
il a	he has
elle a	she has
nous avons	we have
vous avez	you have (polite/plural)
ils ont	they have (masculine)
elles ont	they have (feminine)

13. GRAMMAR INDEX

Here is a list of the principal grammar topics in this course and where to find them in the book.

LOCATION	GRAMMAR TOPICS
Lesson 1 Grammar Builder 1	Informal vs. formal *you* (tu and vous)
Lesson 1 Grammar Builder 2	Review of greetings and introductions
Lesson 2 Grammar Builder 1	Gender (masculine and feminine) and indefinite articles (un and une)
Lesson 2 Grammar Builder 2	Definite articles (le, la, l')
Lesson 3 Grammar Builder 1	Plurals (les and beaucoup de)
Lesson 3 Grammar Builder 2	Subject pronouns (*I, you*, etc.) and être (*to be*)
Lesson 4 Grammar Builder 1	Vocabulary for talking about the home, the word *in*, and il y a (*there is/there are*)
Lesson 4 Grammar Builder 2	Avoir (*to have*)
Lesson 5 Grammar Builder 1	Masculine and feminine forms of adjectives
Lesson 5 Grammar Builder 2	Using adjectives with nouns, plural forms of adjectives, and possessives (*my*, etc.)
Lesson 6 Grammar Builder 1	Question words (*who, what*, etc.), yes/no questions, and negating a verb (*not*)
Lesson 6 Grammar Builder 2	Vocabulary for asking directions and getting around town, and the expression il faut (*you have to, it's necessary to*)
Lesson 7 Grammar Builder 1	*This* and *these*, and using de (*of*) with the definite articles to create *of the* and *some*
Lesson 7 Grammar Builder 2	Polite requests and other ways to ask for things
Lesson 8 Grammar Builder 1	Verbs ending in -er and reflexive verbs (*myself*, etc.)

LOCATION	GRAMMAR TOPICS
Lesson 8 Grammar Builder 2	Faire (*to do*), aller (*to go*), and prendre (*to take*)
Lesson 9 Grammar Builder 1	Professions
Lesson 9 Grammar Builder 2	Telling time and the 24-hour clock
Lesson 10 Grammar Builder 1	Making suggestions, expressing likes and dislikes, and verbs ending in -ir
Lesson 10 Grammar Builder 2	Vouloir (*to want*), pouvoir (*can, to be able*), following a verb with an infinitive, and chez (*at someone's house/place*)

Glossary

Note that the following abbreviations will be used in this glossary:
(m.) = masculine, (f.) = feminine, (sg.) = singular, (pl.) = plural,
(fml.) = formal/polite, (infml.) = informal/familiar. If a word has two
grammatical genders, (m./f.) or (f./m.) is used.

French-English

A

à *in, at, to*
  à la / à l' / au / aux (f./m. or f. before a vowel or
    silent h/m./pl.): *in/at/to the*
  à côté de *next to*
  À votre santé ! *To your health!*
  à plein temps *full-time*
  à temps partiel *part-time*
acheter *to buy*
acteur / actrice (m./f.) *actor/actress*
action (f.) *action*
  film (m.) d'action *action film*
addition (f.) *check, bill*
admirer *to admire*
adolescent / adolescente (m./f.) *teenager,*
  adolescent
adorer *to love, to adore*
adulte (m./f.) *adult*
aéroport (m.) *airport*
affaires (f. pl.) *business, belongings*
  homme / femme (m./f.)
    d'affaires *businessman / businesswoman*
âge (m.) *age*
agneau (m.) *lamb*
agréable *pleasant, enjoyable*
aigre *sour*
aimer *to love, to like*
aller *to go*
  aller visiter *to go sightseeing*
  Allons-y. *Let's go.*
  On y va. *Let's go.* (infml.)
  Comment allez-vous ? *How are you?* (pl./fml.)
  Comment vas-tu ? *How are you?* (infml.)
  Je vais très bien. *I'm very well.*

Allô. *Hello. (only on the phone)*
alors... *well ..., so ..., then ...*
alpinisme (m.) *climbing*
américain / américaine (m./f.) *American*
ami / amie (m./f.) *friend*
amical / amicale (m./f.) *friendly*
amusant / amusante (m./f.) *amusing, funny*
an (m.) *year*
animal (m.) *animal*
année (f.) *year*
anniversaire (m.) *birthday, anniversary*
août *August*
appareil (m.) *device, telephone*
  Qui est à l'appareil ? *Who is it?/Who's*
    calling?
  appareil (m.) photo *camera*
appartement (m.) *apartment*
apporter *to bring*
apprendre *to learn*
  J'apprends le français. *I'm learning French.*
après *after, afterwards*
après-midi (m./f.) *afternoon*
arbre (m.) *tree*
Arc (m.) de Triomphe *Arc de Triomphe (Arch of*
  Triumph)
architecte (m./f.) *architect*
armoire (f.) *wardrobe, cabinet*
  armoire à pharmacie *medicine cabinet*
arrêt (m.) *stop*
  arrêt de bus *bus stop*
arriver *to arrive, to get somewhere, to reach*
art (m.) *art*
artiste (m./f.) *artist*
assez *quite, enough*
assiette (f.) *plate*
assis / assise (m./f.) *sitting (down), seated*
assistant / assistante (m./f.) *assistant*
au *to/at/in the* (m.)

Au revoir. *Good-bye.*
auberge (f.) *inn*
 auberge de jeunesse *youth hostel*
aujourd'hui *today*
aussi *also, too*
autobus (m.) *bus*
autocar (m.) *bus*
automne (m.) *fall, autumn*
 en automne *in (the) fall, in autumn*
autre *other*
 un / une autre (m./f.) *another*
aux *to/at/in the* (pl.)
avant *before*
avec *with*
 Avec plaisir. *With pleasure.*
avenue (f.) *avenue*
avion (m.) *airplane*
avocat / avocate (m./f.) *lawyer*
avoir *to have*
 avoir chaud *to be hot/warm*
 avoir froid *to be cold*
 avoir faim *to be hungry*
 avoir soif *to be thirsty*
 avoir raison *to be right*
 avoir tort *to be wrong*
 avoir honte *to be ashamed*
 avoir peur *to be afraid*
 avoir sommeil *to be sleepy*
 avoir hâte *to look forward to (can't wait)*
avril *April*

B

bague (f.) *ring*
baguette (f.) *baguette (French bread),*
 chopstick
baignoire (f.) *bathtub*
balai (m.) *broom*
balle (f.) *ball (small – tennis, etc.)*
ballet (m.) *ballet*
ballon (m.) *ball (large – basketball, etc.)*
banane (f.) *banana*
bandage (m.) *bandage*
banlieue (f.) *suburbs*
 de banlieue *suburban*
banque (f.) *bank*
banquier / banquière (m./f.) *banker*
bar (m.) *counter, bar*

bas / basse (m./f.) *low*
baseball (m.) *baseball*
basket (m./f.) *sneaker, tennis shoe*
basket(-ball) (m.) *basketball*
bâtiment (m.) *building*
beau / bel / belle (m./m. before vowel or silent h/f.)
 beautiful, handsome, nice
 Il fait beau. *It's beautiful (outside).*
Beaubourg *Beaubourg (area in Paris and an-*
 other name for the Pompidou Center)
beaucoup de *a lot of, many*
beau-fils (m.) *stepson, son-in-law*
beau-père (m.) *father-in-law, stepfather*
bébé (m.) *baby*
belle-fille (f.) *stepdaughter, daughter-in-law*
belle-mère (f.) *mother-in-law, stepmother*
beurre (m.) *butter*
bibliothèque (f.) *library, bookshelf*
bien *well, good, fine, really, very*
 Ça va bien. *It's going well.*
 très bien *very good, very well*
 Bien sûr. *Of course.*
Bienvenue. *Welcome.*
bière (f.) *beer*
bijou (m.) *jewel*
 bijoux (m. pl.) *jewelry*
billard (m.) *pool, billiards*
biologie (f.) *biology*
bisque (f.) *bisque (creamy soup)*
 bisque de homard *lobster bisque*
blanc / blanche (m./f.) *white*
bleu / bleue (m./f.) *blue*
bœuf (m.) *beef*
boire *to drink*
bois (m.) *wood*
 en bois *wooden*
boisson (f.) *drink*
 boisson gazeuse *soft drink*
boîte (f.) *club, nightclub, box*
 boîte de nuit *nightclub*
 sortir en boîte *to go out to clubs, to go out*
 clubbing
 boîte de conserve *can*
 boîte en carton *carton*
bon / bonne (m./f.) *good*
 très bon / bonne (m./f.) *very good*
 Bon appétit. *Bon appetit.*
 Bonne chance. *Good luck.*

Bonjour. *Hello.*
Bonsoir. *Good evening.*
bouche (f.) *mouth*
boucherie (f.) *butcher shop*
boucle (f.) d'oreille *earring*
boulangerie (f.) *bakery*
boulevard (m.) *boulevard*
boulot (m.) *job*
bouteille (f.) *bottle*
bracelet (m.) *bracelet*
bras (m.) *arm*
Bravo. *Well done.*
brochure (f.) *brochure*
brouillard (m.) *fog*
brun / brune (m./f.) *brown*
bulletin (m.) scolaire *report card*
bureau (m.) *office, desk*
  bureau de poste *post office*
bus (m.) *bus*

C

c'est *this is, that is, it is*
  C'est nuageux. *It's cloudy.*
  C'est tout ? *Is that all?*
  Qu'est-ce que c'est ? *What is this/that?*
ça / c' *this, that, it*
  (Comment) ça va ? *How's it going?/How are you?*
  Ça va. *I'm fine./It's going fine.*
  Ça va bien. *It's going well.*
  Ça va mal. *It's not going well./It's going badly.*
  Ça fait... *That makes .../That is ...*
câble (m.) *cable*
café (m.) *café, coffee shop, coffee*
  café-crème (m.) *coffee with cream*
cafetière (f.) *coffeemaker*
cahier (m.) *notebook*
caleçon (m.) *underpants*
calme *quiet, calm*
camper *to go camping*
canadien / canadienne (m./f.) *Canadian*
canapé (m.) *sofa, couch*
canard (m.) *duck*
  canard à l'orange *duck à l'orange, duck with orange sauce*
caramel (m.) *caramel*
carotte (f.) *carrot*

carré (m.) *square, rack (of meat)*
  carré d'agneau *rack of lamb*
carte (f.) *menu, card, map*
  carte des vins *wine list*
  cartes (f. pl.) à jouer *playing cards*
cave (f.) *cellar*
CD-ROM (m.) *CD-ROM*
ce / cet / cette (m./m. before a vowel or silent h/f.) *this, that*
ceinture (f.) *belt*
célèbre *famous*
célébrer *to celebrate*
cent *hundred*
centre (m.) d'informations *information center*
cerveau (m.) *brain*
ces *these, those*
cette / ce / cet (f./m./m. before a vowel or silent h) *this, that*
chacun / chacune (m./f.) *each, each one*
chaîne (f.) hi-fi *sound system*
chaise (f.) *chair*
chambre (f.) (à coucher) *bedroom*
champ (m.) *field*
champion / championne (m./f.) *champion*
changer de chaîne *to change channels*
chanson (f.) *song*
chanter *to sing*
chanteur / chanteuse (m./f.) *singer*
chapeau (m.) *hat*
chaque *each, every*
charmant / charmante (m./f.) *charming*
charpentier (m.) *carpenter*
chaud / chaude (m./f.) *hot, warm*
  Il fait chaud. *It's hot./It's warm.*
  avoir chaud *to be hot/warm*
chauffeur (m.) de taxi *taxi driver*
chaussette (f.) *sock*
chaussure (f.) *shoe*
  chaussure (f.) de basket *sneaker, tennis shoe*
chemise (f.) *shirt*
chemisier (m.) *blouse*
cher / chère (m./f.) *dear, expensive*
chercher *to look for*
cheveux (m. pl.) *hair*
  cheveu (m.) *hair (single strand)*
cheville (f.) *ankle*
chez *at someone's house/place*
chien (m.) *dog*

chimie (f.) *chemistry*
chocolat (m.) *chocolate*
choisir *to choose*
chômage (m.) *unemployment*
　au chômage *unemployed*
chose (f.) *thing*
ci *this, here*
ciel (m.) *sky*
cil (m.) *eyelash*
cinéma (m.) *movie theater, the movies*
cinq *five*
cinquante *fifty*
cinquième *fifth*
circuit (m.) en bus *bus tour*
circulation (f.) *traffic*
cirque (m.) *circus*
clavier (m.) *keyboard*
client / cliente (m./f.) *client*
club (m.) *club (organization)*
cochon (m.) *pig*
cœur (m.) *heart*
coin (m.) *neighborhood, corner*
coïncidence (f.) *coincidence*
　Quelle coïncidence ! *What a coincidence!*
collection (f.) *collection*
collège (m.) *secondary school, junior high school,*
　middle school
collègue / collègue (m./f.) *colleague*
collier (m.) *necklace*
colline (f.) *hill*
combien *how many, how much*
comédie (f.) *comedy*
　comédie romantique *romantic comedy*
comme *like, as, how*
　Comme ci, comme ça. *So-so.*
commencer *to start, to begin*
comment *how*
　Comment ? *Pardon?/What did you say?/How?*
　(Comment) ça va ? *How's it going?/How are*
　　you?
　Comment allez-vous ? *How are you?* (pl./fml.)
　Comment vas-tu ? *How are you?* (infml.)
　Comment vous appelez-vous ? *What's your*
　　name? (pl./fml.)
　Comment t'appelles-tu ?
　　What's your name? (infml.)
compliqué / compliquée (m./f.) *complicated*
comprendre *to understand*

Je ne comprends pas. *I don't understand.*
comptoir (m.) *counter*
concert (m.) *concert*
concombre (m.) *cucumber*
confortable *comfortable*
connaître *to know, to be familiar with*
consommé (m.) *consommé (clear soup made*
　from stock)
　consommé aux vermicelles *noodle soup*
　　(vermicelli pasta consommé)
consulter *to consult*
copain / copine (m./f.) *boyfriend/girlfriend*
costume (m.) *suit*
côte (f.) *chop, rib, coast*
　côte de porc *pork chop*
côté (m.) *side*
　à côté de *next to (at the side of)*
coton (m.) *cotton*
cou (m.) *neck*
coude (m.) *elbow*
couloir (m.) *hall*
courriel (m.) *email*
courrier (m.) électronique *email*
cours (m.) *course, class*
course (f.) *errand, run, race*
　course à pied *running*
court / courte (m./f.) *short*
cousin / cousine (m./f.) *cousin*
couteau (m.) *knife*
crème (f.) *cream, creamy dessert*
　crème à raser *shaving cream*
　crème caramel *creamy dessert made with*
　　caramel
crêpe (f.) *crêpe (tissue-thin pancake)*
　crêpe Suzette *Crêpe Suzette (crêpe with*
　　sugar, orange, and liqueur)
crevettes (f. pl.) *shrimp*
cru / crue (m./f.) *raw*
crudités (f. pl.) *crudités (French appetizer of raw,*
　mixed vegetables)
cuillère (f.) *spoon*
cuir (m.) *leather*
cuisine (f.) *kitchen, cooking*
　faire la cuisine *to do the cooking*
　évier (m.) de la cuisine *kitchen sink*
cuisiner *to cook*
cuisinier / cuisinière (m./f.) *cook*
cuisinière (f.) *stove*

D

D'accord. *Okay./All right.*
dans *in, into*
danse (f.) *dancing, dance*
danser *to dance*
de / d' *of, for, from*
  de la / de l' / du / des (f./m. or f. before a vowel or silent h/m./pl.) *of the, some*
  d'ici *from here*
  De rien. *You're welcome./It's nothing.*
debout *standing (up)*
décembre *December*
décider *to decide*
degré (m.) *degree*
déjà *already*
déjeuner *to have lunch*
déjeuner (m.) *lunch*
délicieux / délicieuse (m./f.) *delicious*
demain *tomorrow*
demander *to ask*
demi / demie (m./f.) *half*
  ... et demie *half past ...*
dent (f.) *tooth*
dentiste (m.) *dentist*
déodorant (m.) *deodorant*
dernier / dernière (m./f.) *last, final, latest, recent*
des *some* (pl.), *of the* (pl.), *plural of un / une*
descendre *to go down, to come down, to descend*
description (f.) *description*
désert (m.) *desert*
dessert (m.) *dessert*
détester *to hate, to detest*
deux *two*
deuxième *second*
devant *in front (of), ahead*
devenir *to become*
devoirs (m. pl.) *homework*
différent / différente (m./f.) *different*
difficile *difficult*
dimanche *Sunday*
dîner *to dine, to have dinner*
dîner (m.) *dinner*
diplôme (m.) *diploma*
  diplôme universitaire *college degree*
directeur / directrice (m./f.) *director, manager*
direction (f.) *direction, way*

divorcer *to get a divorce*
dix *ten*
dix-huit *eighteen*
dixième *tenth*
dix-neuf *nineteen*
dix-sept *seventeen*
docteur (m.) *doctor*
document (m.) *document*
documentaire (m.) *documentary*
doigt (m.) *finger*
  doigt de pied *toe*
donner *to give, to show*
doublé / doublée (m./f.) *dubbed*
douche (f.) *shower*
  gel (m.) **douche** *shower gel*
doux / douce (m./f.) *sweet, soft, gentle*
douze *twelve*
drame (m.) *drama*
drapeau (m.) *flag*
droit *straight*
  tout droit *straight ahead*
droite (f.) *right (opposite of left)*
du / de l' / de la / des (m./m. or f. before a vowel or silent h/f./pl.) *some, of the*

E

eau (f.) *water*
  eau de Cologne *cologne*
  eau de Javel *bleach*
écharpe (f.) *scarf (winter)*
éclair (m.) *lightning*
école (f.) *school*
écouter *to listen (to)*
écran (m.) *monitor, screen*
écrire *to write*
écrivain (m.) (sometimes: **écrivaine**, f.) *writer*
effrayant / effrayante (m./f.) *scary*
église (f.) *church*
électricien (m.) *electrician*
elle *she, it* (f.), *her*
elles *they* (f.), *it* (f. pl.), *them* (f.)
email (m.) *email*
émission (f.) *television program*
emmener *to take along*
emploi (m.) *employment, job*
  emploi régulier *steady job*
  sans emploi *unemployed*

employé / employée (m./f.) *employee*
en *in, into, to, some, of it, of them*
  en effet *really, indeed*
Enchanté. / Enchantée. (m./f.) *Pleased to meet you./Nice to meet you.*
enfant (m./f.) *child*
enfin *finally*
enseignant / enseignante (m./f.) *teacher*
enseigner *to teach*
ensemble *together*
ensuite *then, next*
entraîneur (m.) *coach*
entrée (f.) *appetizer, entrance*
entrer *to enter, to come in*
envoyer *to send, to throw*
  envoyer en pièce jointe *to attach a file*
  envoyer un fichier *to send a file*
  envoyer un mail / mél / email / courriel / courrier électronique *to send an email*
épaule (f.) *shoulder*
épouser (quelqu'un) *to marry (someone)*
équipe (f.) *team*
équitation (f.) *horseback riding*
  faire de l'équitation *to go horseback riding*
escaliers (m. pl.) *stairs*
essentiel / essentielle (m./f.) *essential*
est (m.) *east*
estomac (m.) *stomach, abdomen*
et *and*
étagère (f.) *shelf, bookshelf*
étang (m.) *pond*
été (m.) *summer*
  en été *in (the) summer*
étoile (f.) *star*
être *to be*
étudiant / étudiante (m./f.) *student*
étudier *to study*
eux *them*
évier (m.) *sink*
  évier (m.) de la cuisine *kitchen sink*
exact / exacte (m./f.) *exact, correct*
examen (m.) *test*
  rater (un examen) *to fail (a test)*
  réussir à (un examen) *to pass (a test)*
excellent / excellente (m./f.) *excellent*
excuser *to excuse*
expression (f.) *expression*
extérieur (m.) *outside, exterior*

F

facile *easy*
faible *weak*
faim (f.) *hunger*
  avoir faim *to be hungry*
faire *to do, to make*
  faire la cuisine *to do the cooking*
  faire la lessive *to do the laundry*
  faire la vaisselle *to do the dishes*
  faire le ménage *to do the house cleaning*
  faire les courses *to do the shopping, to go shopping*
  faire un tour *to take/do a tour*
  faire de la marche *to go hiking*
  faire du sport *to play a sport*
  faire match nul *to tie (in a game/match)*
  faire de l'équitation *to go horseback riding*
  faire de la natation *to go swimming*
  faire la queue *to wait in line*
  faire suivre *to forward*
  Ça fait... *That makes .../That is ...*
  Il fait beau. *It's beautiful (outside).*
  Il fait chaud. *It's hot./It's warm.*
  Il fait froid. *It's cold.*
  Il fait (du) soleil. *It's sunny.*
  Il fait du vent. *It's windy.*
falloir *to be necessary*
  il faut *it's necessary to, you have/need to, you must*
famille (f.) *family*
fauteuil (m.) *armchair*
faux / fausse (m./f.) *false, wrong*
Félicitations. *Congratulations.*
femme (f.) *woman, wife*
  femme d'affaires *businesswoman*
fenêtre (f.) *window*
fer (m.) à repasser *iron*
fermer *to close*
  fermer un fichier *to close a file*
fermier / fermière (m./f.) *farmer*
fête (f.) *party, festival, holiday*
feu (m.) *fire*
février *February*
fiancé / fiancée (m./f.) *fiancé/fiancée*
fichier (m.) *file*
fille (f.) *girl, daughter*
  fille unique *only child* (f.)

film (m.) *movie, film*
  film d'action *action film*
  film policier *crime drama/film, detective drama/film*
fils (m.) *son*
  fils unique *only child* (m.)
finir *to finish*
firme (f.) *company, firm*
fleur (f.) *flower*
fois (f.) *time*
  une fois *once (one time)*
foot(ball) (m.) *soccer*
football (m.) américain *(American) football*
footballeur / footballeuse (m./f.) *soccer player*
forêt (f.) *forest*
Formidable. *Fantastic.*
fort / forte (m./f.) *strong*
foulard (m.) *scarf (fashion)*
four (m.) *oven*
fourchette (f.) *fork*
foyer (m.) *home*
français (m.) *French language*
français / française (m./f.) *French*
frère (m.) *brother*
frites (f. pl.) *French fries*
froid / froide (m./f.) *cold*
  Il fait froid. *It's cold.*
  avoir froid *to be cold*
fromage (m.) *cheese*
front (m.) *forehead*
fruit (m.) *fruit*

G

gagner *to win, to earn*
galerie (f.) *gallery*
gant (m.) *glove*
garage (m.) *garage*
garçon (m.) *boy*
gare (f.) *train station*
gâteau (m.) *cake*
gauche (f.) *left*
gel (m.) douche *shower gel*
généreux / généreuse (m./f.) *generous*
genou (m.) *knee*
gens (m. pl.) *people*
gentil / gentille (m./f.) *nice, kind*
gérant / gérante (m./f.) *manager*

goût (m.) *taste*
grammaire (f.) *grammar*
grand / grande (m./f.) *big, large, tall*
  grand magasin (m.) *department store*
grand-mère (f.) *grandmother*
grand-parent (m.) *grandparent*
grand-père (m.) *grandfather*
grêle (f.) *hail*
  Il grêle. *It's hailing.*
gros / grosse (m./f.) *fat*
groupe (m.) de musique *band*
guide (m.) *guide*
gymnastique (f.) *gym (physical education), gymnastics*

H

habiter *to live*
haine (f.) *hatred*
haltérophilie (f.) *weight lifting*
haricot (m.) *bean*
  haricot vert *green bean*
hasard (m.) *chance*
hâte (f.) *haste*
  avoir hâte *to look forward to (can't wait)*
hâter *to hasten*
  se hâter *to rush*
haut / haute (m./f.) *high*
hériter *to inherit*
héros / héroïne (m./f.) *hero / heroine*
heure (f.) *hour*
  Quelle heure est-il ? *What time is it?*
heureux / heureuse (m./f.) *happy*
hier *yesterday*
histoire (f.) *history, story*
hiver (m.) *winter*
  en hiver *in (the) winter*
hockey (m.) *hockey*
homard (m.) *lobster*
homme (m.) *man*
  homme d'affaires *businessman*
honte (f.) *shame*
  avoir honte *to be ashamed*
hôpital (m.) *hospital*
horaire (m.) *schedule*
hors *outside (of)*
hors-d'œuvre (m.) *appetizer*
hôtel (m.) *hotel*

huile (f.) *oil*
huit *eight*
huitième *eighth*

I

ici *here*
  d'ici *from here*
  par ici *this way*
idée (f.) *idea*
il *he, it* (m.)
  Il fait beau. *It's beautiful (outside).*
  Il fait chaud. *It's hot./It's warm.*
  Il fait froid. *It's cold.*
  Il fait (du) soleil. *It's sunny.*
  Il fait du vent. *It's windy.*
  Il grêle. *It's hailing.*
  Il neige. *It's snowing.*
  Il pleut. *It's raining./It rains.*
  il faut *it's necessary to, you have/need to, you must*
il y a *there is/are*
  Il y a du vent. *It's windy.*
Île (f.) de la Cité *Île de la Cité (City Island)*
ils *they* (m./mixed), *it* (m. pl.)
immeuble (m.) *apartment building*
imprimante (f.) *printer*
ingénieur (m.) *engineer*
intelligent / intelligente (m./f.) *intelligent*
intéressant / intéressante (m./f.) *interesting*
Internet (m.) *internet*
intersection (f.) *intersection*
inviter *to invite*

J

jamais *never*
jambe (f.) *leg*
janvier *January*
jardin (m.) *garden*
jaune *yellow*
je / j' *I*
  Je m'appelle... *My name is ... /I am called ...*
  Je ne comprends pas. *I don't understand.*
  Je vais très bien. *I'm very well.*
  Je veux... *I want ...*
  Je voudrais... *I would like ...*
  Je te présente... / Je vous présente...

  Let me introduce ... (infml./pl., fml.)
  Je vous en prie. *You're welcome.* (fml.)
jean (m.) *jeans*
jeu (m.) *game*
  jeu électronique *electronic game*
  jeu vidéo *video game*
jeudi *Thursday*
jeune *young*
Joconde (f.) *Mona Lisa*
joli / jolie (m./f.) *nice, pretty*
joue (f.) *cheek*
jouer *to play, to perform, to act*
  cartes (f. pl.) à jouer *playing cards*
joueur / joueuse (m./f.) *player (games, sports, etc.)*
jour (m.) *day*
journaliste (m./f.) *journalist*
journée (f.) *day*
juillet *July*
juin *June*
jupe (f.) *skirt*
jus (m.) *juice*
jusqu'à *to, until, up to, up until*

L

là *there*
la / l' / le / les (f./m. or f. before a vowel or silent h/m./pl.) *the*
là-bas *over there, there*
lac (m.) *lake*
laid / laide (m./f.) *ugly*
lait (m.) *milk*
laitue (f.) *lettuce*
lampadaire (m.) *streetlight*
lampe (f.) *lamp*
langue (f.) *language, tongue*
lave-linge (m.) *washing machine*
laver *to wash*
  se laver *to wash up, to wash oneself*
lave-vaisselle (m.) *dishwasher*
le / l' / la / les (m./m. or f. before a vowel or silent h/f./pl.) *the*
leçon (f.) *lesson*
lecteur (m.) *player (CDs, DVDs, etc.), drive (computer)*
  lecteur de CD *CD player*
  lecteur de DVD *DVD player*

lecteur de CD-ROM *CD-ROM drive*
légume (m.) *vegetable*
lent / lente (m./f.) *slow*
lentement *slowly*
les *the* (pl.)
lessive (f.) *laundry detergent*
lettre (f.) *letter*
leur / leurs (m. or f./pl.) *their*
liaison (f.) *link*
librairie (f.) *bookstore*
liquide (m.) vaisselle *dishwashing detergent*
lire *to read*
lit (m.) *bed*
littérature (f.) *literature*
livre (m.) *book*
  livre scolaire *textbook*
loin *far*
  loin d'ici *far from here*
  plus loin *farther*
long / longue (m./f.) *long*
Louvre (m.) *Louvre*
lui *him*
lundi *Monday*
lune (f.) *moon*
lunettes (f. pl.) *eyeglasses*
  lunettes de soleil *sunglasses*
lustre (m.) *chandelier*

M

ma / mon / mes (f./m./pl.) *my*
machine (f.) à laver *washing machine*
madame *ma'am, Mrs., Ms., madam*
mademoiselle *miss*
magasin (m.) *store*
  grand magasin *department store*
  magasin d'électronique *electronics store*
  magasin de chaussures *shoe store*
  magasin de vêtements *clothing store*
magazine (m.) *magazine*
mai *May*
mail (m.) *email*
maillot (m.) de bain *bathing suit, bathing trunks*
maillot (m.) de corps *undershirt*
main (f.) *hand*
maintenant *now*
maire (m.) *mayor*
mairie (f.) *city hall, municipal building*

mais *but*
maison *homemade*
maison (f.) *house, home*
mal *badly, bad, wrong*
  Ça va mal. *It's going badly./It's not going well.*
malade *sick*
maman *Mom, Mommy*
manger *to eat*
manteau (m.) *coat*
marché (m.) *market*
mardi *Tuesday*
mare (f.) *pond*
mari (m.) *husband*
marron *brown*
mars *March*
match (m.) *match, game*
mathématiques (f.) *math*
maths (f.) *math*
matin (m.) *morning*
matinée (f.) *morning*
mauvais / mauvaise (m./f.) *bad*
me / m' (reflexive pronoun): *myself*
  Je m'appelle... *My name is .../I am called ...*
médecin (m.) *doctor*
médecine (f.) *medicine*
mél (m.) *email*
melon (m.) *melon*
même *same, even*
mémoire (f.) *memory*
ménage (m.) *house cleaning*
menton (m.) *chin*
menu (m.) *menu*
mer (f.) *sea*
merci *thank you*
mercredi *Wednesday*
mère (f.) *mother*
mes / mon / ma (pl./m./f.) *my*
message (m.) instantané *instant message*
métro (m.) *subway, metro*
mettre *to put*
  mettre à la poste *to mail, to put in the mail*
micro-ondes (m.) *microwave (oven)*
midi (m.) *noon*
miel (m.) *honey*
mille *thousand*
mince *thin*
minuit (m.) *midnight*
miroir (m.) *mirror*

mixer (m.) *blender*
modem (m.) *modem*
moi *me*
moins *less, minus*
  ... moins le quart *quarter to ...*
mois (m.) *month*
moment (m.) *moment*
mon / ma / mes (m./f./pl.) *my*
monsieur *sir, Mr.*
montagne (f.) *mountain*
monter *to go up, to come up, to rise*
montre (f.) *watch*
montrer *to show*
monument (m.) *monument*
moquette (f.) *carpet*
mosquée (f.) *mosque*
mot (m.) *word*
moto (f.) *motorcycling, motorcycle*
mousse (f.) *mousse*
mur (m.) *wall*
muscle (m.) *muscle*
musée (m.) *museum*
musicien / musicienne (m./f.) *musician*
musique (f.) *music*
mystérieux / mystérieuse (m./f.) *mysterious*

N

natation (f.) *swimming*
  faire de la natation *to go swimming*
ne / n'... pas *not*
  n'est-ce pas ? *isn't it?, isn't that so?, right?*
neige (f.) *snow*
neiger *to snow*
  Il neige. *It's snowing.*
neuf *nine*
neuvième *ninth*
neveu (m.) *nephew*
nez (m.) *nose*
nièce (f.) *niece*
noir / noire (m./f.) *black*
nom (m.) *name*
nombre (m.) *number*
non *no*
nord (m.) *north*
note (f.) *grade, note*
notre / nos (m. or f./pl.) *our*
nourriture (f.) *food*

nous *we, us*
nous (reflexive pronoun): *ourselves*
nouveau / nouvel / nouvelle (m./m. before a
  vowel or silent h/f.) *new*
nouvelles (f. pl.) *news (the news)*
novembre *November*
nuage (m.) *cloud*
nuageux / nuageuse (m./f.) *cloudy*
  C'est nuageux. *It's cloudy.*
nuit (f.) *night*

O

occupé / occupée (m./f.) *busy*
océan (m.) *ocean*
octobre *October*
œil (m.) (yeux, pl.) *eye (eyes)*
œuf (m.) *egg*
oignon (m.) *onion*
on *we* (infml.), *people in general, one (pronoun)*
  On y va. *Let's go.* (infml.)
oncle (m.) *uncle*
onze *eleven*
opéra (m.) *opera*
orage (m.) *storm*
orange (f.) *orange*
ordinateur (m.) *computer*
oreille (f.) *ear*
organiser *to organize*
  organiser une fête *to have a party*
original / originale (m./f.) *original*
orteil (m.) *toe*
os (m.) *bone*
ou *or*
où *where*
  Où se trouve... ? / Où est... ? *Where is ... ?*
  Où sont les toilettes ? *Where is the restroom?*
ouest (m.) *west*
oui *yes*
ouragan (m.) *hurricane*
ouvrier (m.) en bâtiment *construction worker*
ouvrir *to open*
  ouvrir un fichier *to open a file*

P

page (f.) web *webpage*
pain (m.) *bread*

pansement (m.) *bandage*
pantalon (m.) *pants*
papa *Dad, Daddy*
papier (m.) hygiénique *toilet paper*
parapluie (m.) *umbrella*
parc (m.) *park*
Pardon. *Pardon (me)./Excuse me.*
parent (m.) *relative, parent*
parfait / parfaite (m./f.) *perfect*
parfois *sometimes*
parfum (m.) *perfume, flavor*
Paris *Paris*
parler *to speak, to talk*
  Parlez plus lentement, s'il vous plaît. *Speak more slowly, please.*
  Je parle un peu français. *I speak a little French.*
partie (f.) *party*
partir *to leave, to go away*
pas *not*
  Pas mal. *Not bad.*
passeport (m.) *passport*
passer *to pass, to go (past)*
passionnant / passionnante (m./f.) *exciting*
pâté (m.) *pâté (spreadable purée of meat)*
patin (m.) *skating, skate*
  patin à glace *ice skating, ice skate*
pâtisserie (f.) *pastry shop, pastry*
patron / patronne (m./f.) *boss*
pauvre *poor, impoverished*
payer *to pay*
peau (f.) *skin*
pêche (f.) *peach*
  pêche Melba *peaches with ice cream*
peindre *to paint*
pendule (f.) *grandfather clock*
penser *to think*
perdre *to lose*
perdu / perdue (m./f.) *lost*
  Je suis perdu / perdue. *I'm lost.*
père (m.) *father*
personne (f.) *person*
personnel (m.) *staff*
petit / petite (m./f.) *small, little, short*
  petit ami / petite amie (m./f.) *boyfriend/ girlfriend*
  petit déjeuner (m.) *breakfast*
  prendre le petit déjeuner *to have breakfast*

peu amical / peu amicale (m./f.) *unfriendly*
pharmacie (f.) *pharmacy, drugstore*
photo (f.) *photo*
  Pourriez-vous nous prendre en photo, s'il vous plaît ? *Can you take our picture (photo), please?*
pièce (f.) *room, play (theater), piece*
  pièce jointe *attachment*
pied (m.) *foot*
placard (m.) *cupboard, closet*
place (f.) *place, seat, ticket, room*
plafond (m.) *ceiling*
plage (f.) *beach*
plaisir (m.) *pleasure*
  Avec plaisir. *With pleasure.*
plan (m.) *map*
planche (f.) à repasser *ironing board*
plante (f.) *plant*
plastique (m.) *plastic*
  en plastique *made of plastic*
plat (m.) *dish*
plat principal *main dish/course*
pleuvoir *to rain*
  Il pleut. *It's raining./It rains.*
plombier (m.) *plumber*
pluie (f.) *rain*
plus *more*
  plus loin *farther*
poignet (m.) *wrist*
poire (f.) *pear*
poisson (m.) *fish*
poitrine (f.) *chest*
poivre (m.) *pepper (condiment)*
poivron (m.) *pepper (vegetable)*
policier / femme policier (m./f.) *policeman/woman*
policier / policière (m./f.) *police, detective (adjective)*
  film (m.) policier *detective drama/film, crime drama/film*
pomme (f.) *apple*
  pomme de terre *potato*
pont (m.) *bridge*
porc (m.) *pork, pig*
porte (f.) *door*
porter *to carry, to wear*
poste (f.) *post office, mail*
  bureau (m.) de poste *post office*

mettre à la poste *to mail, to put in the mail*
poudre (f.) *powder*
poulet (m.) *chicken*
poumon (m.) *lung*
pour *for, to*
pouvoir *can, to be able*
pratiquer *to practice*
préféré / préférée (m./f.) *favorite*
préférer *to prefer*
premier / première (m./f.) *first*
prendre *to take, to have (food/drink)*
  prendre un bain *to take a bath*
  prendre une douche *to take a shower*
  prendre un verre *to have a drink*
  prendre le petit déjeuner *to have breakfast*
  prendre une chambre *to check in*
  prendre une photo *to take a picture (photo)*
  Pourriez-vous nous prendre en photo, s'il vous plaît ? *Can you take our picture (photo) please?*
préparer *to prepare, to make, to cook*
près *close, near*
  tout près *very close, very near*
  près d'ici *nearby, near here, close to here*
présenter *to introduce, to show, to present*
  Je te présente… / Je vous présente… *Let me introduce …* (infml./pl., fml.)
prêt / prête (m./f.) *ready*
prier *to beg*
  Je vous en prie. *You're welcome.* (fml.)
printemps (m.) *spring*
  au printemps *in (the) spring*
prof (m./f.) *professor, teacher* (infml.)
professeur / professeure (m./f.) *professor, teacher*
progrès (m.) *progress*
propre *clean, own*
puis *then*
pyjama (m.) *pajamas*

Q

qu'est-ce que *what*
  Qu'est-ce que c'est ? *What is this/that?*
quarante *forty*
quart (m.) *quarter*
  … et quart *quarter after/past …*
  … moins le quart *quarter to …*

quartier (m.) *neighborhood*
quatorze *fourteen*
quatre *four*
quatre-vingt-dix *ninety*
quatre-vingts *eighty*
quatrième *fourth*
que *what, that, which, whom*
quel / quelle (m./f.) *which, what*
  Quel temps fait-il aujourd'hui ? *What is the weather today?*
  Quelle heure est-il ? *What time is it?*
queue (f.) *line, tail*
  faire la queue *to wait in line*
qui *who, that*
  Qui est à l'appareil ? *Who is it?/Who's calling?*
quiche (f.) *quiche*
  quiche lorraine *type of quiche made with bacon*
quinze *fifteen*
quoi *what*
quotidien / quotidienne (m./f.) *everyday, daily*

R

radis (m.) *radish*
raisin (m.) *grape(s)*
rasoir (m.) *razor*
rater (un examen) *to fail (a test)*
réception (f.) *reception desk*
récré(ation) (f.) *recess*
réfrigérateur (m.) *refrigerator*
regarder *to watch*
régler sa note *to check out*
rencontrer (une personne/quelqu'un) *to meet (a person/someone)*
rendez-vous (m.) *meeting, appointment*
rentrer *to go home, to return, to come back (in), to go in*
répéter *to repeat*
  Répétez, s'il vous plaît. *Repeat (that), please.*
répondre *to reply*
réservation (f.) *reservation*
réserver *to reserve*
restaurant (m.) *restaurant*
rester *to stay*
retraite (f.) *retirement*
  à la retraite *retired*

réunion (f.) *meeting, reunion*
réussir à (un examen) *to succeed, to pass (a test)*
revenir *to come back, to return*
réverbère (m.) *lamppost*
revue (f.) *magazine*
riche *rich*
rideau (m.) *curtain*
rien *nothing, anything*
   De rien. *You're welcome./It's nothing.*
rivière (f.) *river*
riz (m.) *rice*
robe (f.) *dress*
rocher (m.) *rock*
rôle (m.) *role, part (in a play, movie, etc.)*
romantique *romantic*
rôti (m.) *roast, joint (of meat)*
rôti / rôtie (m./f.) *roast(ed)*
rouge *red*
rue (f.) *street*
rural / rurale (m./f.) *rural*

S

s'amuser *to have fun, to have a good time*
s'appeler *to be called*
   Comment vous appelez-vous ? *What's your name?* (pl./fml.)
   Comment t'appelles-tu ? *What's your name?* (infml.)
   Je m'appelle... *My name is ... / I am called ...*
s'ennuyer *to be bored*
s'habiller *to get dressed, to dress oneself*
s'il te plaît / s'il vous plaît *please* (infml./pl., fml.)
sa / son / ses (f./m./pl.) *his, her, its*
sable (m.) *sand*
Sacré-Cœur (m.) *Sacré Cœur (Sacred Heart)*
salade (f.) *salad*
   salade de fruits *fruit salad*
saladier (m.) *bowl*
salaire (m.) *salary*
sale *dirty*
salle (f.) *room, hall*
   salle à manger *dining room*
   salle de bains *bathroom, washroom*
   salle de classe *classroom*
   salle de réunion *meeting room*
salon (m.) *living room*
Salut. *Hi./Bye.*

samedi *Saturday*
sang (m.) *blood*
sans *without*
santé (f.) *health*
   À votre santé ! *To your health!*
   en bonne santé *healthy*
sardines (f. pl.) *sardines*
   sardines sauce tomate *sardines in tomato sauce*
sauce (f.) *sauce*
sauvegarder un document *to save a document*
savoir *to know*
savon (m.) *soap*
sculpture (f.) *sculpture*
se / s' (reflexive pronoun): *himself, herself, itself, themselves, oneself*
   s'amuser *to have fun, to have a good time*
   s'appeler *to be called*
   s'ennuyer *to be bored*
   s'habiller *to get dressed, to dress oneself*
   se coucher *to go to bed*
   se hâter *to rush*
   se laver *to wash up, to wash oneself*
   se lever *to get up*
   se raser *to shave*
   se trouver *to find oneself (somewhere), to be situated*
sèche-linge (m.) *dryer*
second / seconde (m./f.) *second*
secrétaire (m./f.) *secretary*
seize *sixteen*
sel (m.) *salt*
semaine (f.) *week*
sept *seven*
septembre *September*
septième *seventh*
serveur / serveuse (m./f.) *waiter/waitress, server*
serviette (f.) *napkin, towel, briefcase*
   serviette de bain *bath towel*
ses / son / sa (pl./m./f.) *his, her, its*
shampooing (m.) *shampoo*
si *if, yes (negative)*
site (m.) web *website*
six *six*
sixième *sixth*
ski (m.) *skiing*
social / sociale (m./f.) *social*

société (f.) *company*
sœur (f.) *sister*
soie (f.) *silk*
soif (f.) *thirst*
  avoir soif *to be thirsty*
soir (m.) *evening, night*
  ce soir *tonight, this evening*
soirée (f.) *party, evening*
soixante *sixty*
soixante-dix *seventy*
sol (m.) *floor*
sole (f.) *sole (fish)*
  sole meunière *sole covered in flour and sau-*
    téed in butter
soleil (m.) *sun*
  Il fait (du) soleil. *It's sunny.*
son / sa / ses (m./f./pl.) *his, her, its*
sortir *to leave, to go out*
  sortir en boîte *to go out to clubs, to go out*
    clubbing
soupe (f.) *soup*
  soupe à l'oignon *onion soup*
sourcil (m.) *eyebrow*
sourire (m.) *smile*
souris (f.) *mouse*
sous-titre (m.) *subtitle*
sous-vêtements (m. pl.) *underwear*
spécialité (f.) *specialty*
sportif / sportive (m./f.) *athletic*
sports (m. pl.) *sports*
stade (m.) *stadium*
  stade de foot *soccer stadium*
station (f.) *station*
  station de métro *subway station, metro sta-*
    tion
statue (f.) *statue*
sucre (m.) *sugar*
sud (m.) *south*
suisse *Swiss*
sujet (m.) *subject*
Super. *Super./Great.*
supermarché (m.) *supermarket*
supprimer *to delete*
surtout *mostly, above all, especially*
sympa *cool, nice, good*
  très sympa *very cool/nice/good*
synagogue (f.) *synagogue*

T

ta / ton / tes (f./m./pl.) *your* (infml.)
table (f.) *table*
  table pour deux *table for two*
tableau (m.) *painting*
taille (f.) *size*
talc (m.) *powder*
talentueux / talentueuse (m./f.) *talented*
tante (f.) *aunt*
tasse (f.) *cup*
taxi (m.) *taxi, cab*
te / t' (reflexive pronoun) *yourself* (infml.)
télé(vision) (f.) *television, TV*
télécopieur (m.) *fax machine*
téléphone (m.) *telephone*
téléphoner *to phone, to call, to make a phone call*
température (f.) *temperature*
temple (m.) *temple*
temps (m.) *weather, time*
  Quel temps fait-il aujourd'hui ? *What is the*
    weather today?
tendon (m.) *tendon*
tennis (m.) *tennis*
terminer *to finish, to end*
terre (f.) *land*
tes / ton / ta (pl./m./f.) *your* (infml.)
tête (f.) *head*
thé (m.) *tea*
théâtre (m.) *theater*
théière (f.) *teakettle, teapot*
timbre (m.) *stamp*
tiroir (m.) *drawer*
toi *you* (infml.)
toilettes (f. pl.) *toilet, restroom*
  Où sont les toilettes ? *Where is the restroom?*
tomate (f.) *tomato*
tomber *to fall*
ton / ta / tes (m./f./pl.) *your* (infml.)
tonnerre (m.) *thunder*
toujours *always, still*
tour (f.) *tower*
  Tour Eiffel *Eiffel Tower*
tour (m.) *tour, turn*
touriste (m./f.) *tourist*
tourner *to turn*
tout / toute (m./f.) *all, every*
  C'est tout ? *Is that all?*

train (m.) *train*
travail (m.) *work*
travailler *to work*
traverser *to cross, to go across*
treize *thirteen*
trente *thirty*
très *very*
  très bien *very good, very well*
  très bon / bonne *very good*
triste *sad*
trois *three*
troisième *third*
trottoir (m.) *sidewalk*
trouver *to find*
  se trouver *to find oneself (somewhere), to be situated*
  Où se trouve... ? *Where is ... ?*
truite (f.) *trout*
  truite au bleu *trout cooked in wine and vinegar*
T-shirt (m.) *T-shirt*
tu *you* (infml.)

U

un / une (m./f.) (plural of un / une is des) *a, an, one*
  un peu *a little*
université (f.) *university, college*
urbain / urbaine (m./f.) *urban*
usine (f.) *factory*

V

vacances (f. pl.) *vacation*
vain / vaine (m./f.) *vain*
vélo (m.) *bike*
vendeur / vendeuse (m./f.) *salesman/woman*
vendre *to sell*
vendredi *Friday*
venir *to come*
vent (m.) *wind*
  Il fait du vent. / Il y a du vent. *It's windy.*
vermicelle (m.) *vermicelli pasta*
  consommé (m.) aux vermicelles *noodle soup (vermicelli pasta consommé)*
verre (m.) *glass*
  prendre un verre *to have a drink*

version (f.) *version*
  version française (v.f.) *French version of a film (dubbed into French)*
  version originale (v.o.) *original version of a film (not dubbed into French)*
veste (f.) *jacket*
vêtements (m. pl.) *clothes, clothing*
vétérinaire (m.) *veterinarian*
viande (f.) *meat*
vie (f.) *life*
vietnamien / vietnamienne (m./f.) *Vietnamese*
vieux / vieil / vieille (m./m. before a vowel or silent h/f.) *old*
village (m.) *village*
ville (f.) *town, city*
vin (m.) *wine*
  vin rouge / blanc / rosé *red/white/rosé wine*
vingt *twenty*
violet / violette (m./f.) *purple*
violon (m.) *violin*
visage (m.) *face*
visite (f.) guidée *guided tour*
visiter *to visit (a place)*
vocabulaire (m.) *vocabulary*
voici *here is/are, here it is/they are*
voilà *there is/are, here is/are, there it is/they are, here it is/they are*
voile (f.) *sailing*
voir *to see*
voiture (f.) *car*
votre / vos (m. or f./pl.) *your* (pl./fml.)
vouloir *to want*
  Je veux... *I want ...*
  Je voudrais... *I would like ...*
vous *you* (pl./fml.)
vous (reflexive pronoun) *yourself* (fml.), *yourselves*
voyager *to travel*
vrai / vraie (m./f.) *true, real*

W

wagon (m.) *car (on a train)*
  wagon-lit (m.) *sleeping/sleeper car*
week-end (m.) *weekend*

Y

yeux (m. pl.) (*œil, sg.*) *eyes* (eye)

Z

zéro *zero*

English-French

A

a, an *un / une* (m./f.) (plural of *un / une* is des)
  a little *un peu*
  a lot of *beaucoup de*
abdomen *estomac* (m.)
able (to be) *pouvoir*
above all *surtout*
act (to) *jouer*
action *action* (f.)
  action film *film* (m.) *d'action*
actor/actress *acteur / actrice* (m./f.)
admire (to) *admirer*
adolescent *adolescent / adolescente* (m./f.)
adore (to) *adorer*
adult *adulte* (m./f.)
afraid (to be) *avoir peur*
after *après*
afternoon *après-midi* (m./f.)
afterwards *après*
age *âge* (m.)
ahead *devant*
airplane *avion* (m.)
airport *aéroport* (m.)
all *tout / toute* (m./f.)
  All right. *D'accord.*
  Is that all? *C'est tout ?*
already *déjà*
also *aussi*
always *toujours*
American *américain / américaine* (m./f.)
amusing *amusant / amusante* (m./f.)
and *et*
animal *animal* (m.)
ankle *cheville* (f.)
anniversary *anniversaire* (m.)
another *un / une autre* (m./f.)

anything *rien*
apartment *appartement* (m.)
  apartment building *immeuble* (m.)
appetizer *entrée* (f.), *hors-d'œuvre* (m.)
apple *pomme* (f.)
appointment *rendez-vous* (m.)
April *avril*
Arc de Triomphe (Arch of Triumph) *Arc* (m.) *de Triomphe*
architect *architecte* (m./f.)
arm *bras* (m.)
armchair *fauteuil* (m.)
arrive (to) *arriver*
art *art* (m.)
artist *artiste* (m./f.)
as *comme*
ashamed (to be) *avoir honte*
ask (to) *demander*
assistant *assistant / assistante* (m./f.)
at *à*
  at the *au / à la / à l' / aux* (m./f./m. or f. before a vowel or silent h/pl.)
  at someone's house/place *chez*
athletic *sportif / sportive* (m./f.)
attach a file (to) *envoyer en pièce jointe*
attachment *pièce* (f.) *jointe*
August *août*
aunt *tante* (f.)
autumn *automne* (m.)
  in autumn *en automne*
avenue *avenue* (f.)

B

baby *bébé* (m.)
bad *mauvais / mauvaise* (m./f.), *mal*
badly *mal*
  It's going badly./It's not going well. *Ça va mal.*
baguette (French bread) *baguette* (f.)
bakery *boulangerie* (f.)
ball (large – basketball, etc.) *ballon* (m.)
ball (small – tennis, etc.) *balle* (f.)
ballet *ballet* (m.)
banana *banane* (f.)
band *groupe* (m.) *de musique*
bandage *bandage* (m.), *pansement* (m.)
bank *banque* (f.)

banker *banquier / banquière* (m./f.)
baseball *baseball* (m.)
basketball *basket(-ball)* (m.)
bath towel *serviette* (f.) *de bain*
bathing suit *maillot* (m.) *de bain*
bathing trunks *maillot* (m.) *de bain*
bathroom *salle* (f.) *de bains*
bathtub *baignoire* (f.)
be (to) *être*
  be able (to) *pouvoir*
  be afraid (to) *avoir peur*
  be ashamed (to) *avoir honte*
  be bored (to) *s'ennuyer*
  be cold (to) *avoir froid*
  be hot/warm (to) *avoir chaud*
  be hungry (to) *avoir faim*
  be thirsty (to) *avoir soif*
  be sleepy (to) *avoir sommeil*
  be right (to) *avoir raison*
  be wrong (to) *avoir tort*
  be familiar with (to) *connaître*
  be situated (to) *se trouver*
  be called (to) *s'appeler*
  be necessary (to) *falloir*
beach *plage* (f.)
bean *haricot* (m.)
  green bean *haricot vert*
Beaubourg (area in Paris and another name
  for the Pompidou Center) *Beaubourg*
beautiful *beau / bel / belle* (m./m. before vowel or
  silent h/f.)
  It's beautiful (outside). *Il fait beau.*
become (to) *devenir*
bed *lit* (m.)
bedroom *chambre* (f.) *(à coucher)*
beef *bœuf* (m.)
beer *bière* (f.)
before *avant*
beg (to) *prier*
begin (to) *commencer*
belongings *affaires* (f. pl.)
belt *ceinture* (f.)
big *grand / grande* (m./f.)
bike *vélo* (m.)
bill (restaurant, café, etc.) *addition* (f.)
billiards *billard* (m.)
biology *biologie* (f.)
birthday *anniversaire* (m.)

bisque (creamy soup) *bisque* (f.)
  lobster bisque *bisque de homard*
black *noir / noire* (m./f.)
bleach *eau* (f.) *de Javel*
blender *mixer* (m.)
blood *sang* (m.)
blouse *chemisier* (m.)
blue *bleu / bleue* (m./f.)
Bon appetit. *Bon appétit.*
bone *os* (m.)
book *livre* (m.)
bookshelf *étagère* (f.), *bibliothèque* (f.)
bookstore *librairie* (f.)
bored (to be) *s'ennuyer*
boss *patron / patronne* (m./f.)
bottle *bouteille* (f.)
boulevard *boulevard* (m.)
bowl *saladier* (m.)
box *boîte* (f.)
boy *garçon* (m.)
boyfriend *copain* (m.), *petit ami* (m.)
bracelet *bracelet* (m.)
brain *cerveau* (m.)
bread *pain* (m.)
breakfast *petit déjeuner* (m.)
  have breakfast (to) *prendre le petit déjeuner*
bridge *pont* (m.)
briefcase *serviette* (f.)
bring (to) *apporter*
brochure *brochure* (f.)
broom *balai* (m.)
brother *frère* (m.)
brown *marron, brun / brune* (m./f.)
building *bâtiment* (m.)
bus *bus* (m.), *autobus* (m.), *autocar* (m.)
  bus stop *arrêt* (m.) *de bus*
  bus tour *circuit* (m.) *en bus*
business *affaires* (f. pl.)
businessman/woman *homme / femme*
  d'affaires (m./f.)
busy *occupé / occupée* (m./f.)
but *mais*
butcher shop *boucherie* (f.)
butter *beurre* (m.)
buy (to) *acheter*
Bye. *Salut.*

C

cab *taxi* (m.)
cabinet *armoire* (f.)
  medicine cabinet *armoire à pharmacie*
cable *câble* (m.)
café *café* (m.)
cake *gâteau* (m.)
call (to) *téléphoner*
called (to be) *s'appeler*
calm *calme*
camera *appareil* (m.) *photo*
can (container) *boîte* (f.) *de conserve*
can (verb) *pouvoir*
Canadian *canadien / canadienne* (m./f.)
car *voiture* (f.), *wagon (on a train)* (m.)
caramel *caramel* (m.)
card *carte* (f.)
  playing cards *cartes* (f. pl.) *à jouer*
carpenter *charpentier* (m.)
carpet *moquette* (f.)
carrot *carotte* (f.)
carry (to) *porter*
carton *boîte* (f.) *en carton*
CD player *lecteur* (m.) *de CD*
CD-ROM *CD-ROM* (m.)
  CD-ROM drive *lecteur* (m.) *de CD-ROM*
ceiling *plafond* (m.)
celebrate (to) *célébrer*
cellar *cave* (f.)
chair *chaise* (f.)
champion *champion / championne* (m./f.)
chance *hasard* (m.)
chandelier *lustre* (m.)
change channels (to) *changer de chaîne*
charming *charmant / charmante* (m./f.)
check (restaurant, café, etc.) *addition* (f.)
check in (to) *prendre une chambre*
check out (to) *régler sa note*
cheek *joue* (f.)
cheese *fromage* (m.)
chemistry *chimie* (f.)
chest *poitrine* (f.)
chicken *poulet* (m.)
child *enfant* (m./f.)
chin *menton* (m.)
chocolate *chocolat* (m.)
choose (to) *choisir*

chop *côte* (f.)
  pork chop *côte de porc*
chopstick *baguette* (f.)
church *église* (f.)
circus *cirque* (m.)
city *ville* (f.)
  city hall *mairie* (f.)
class *cours* (m.)
classroom *salle* (f.) *de classe*
clean *propre*
client *client / cliente* (m./f.)
climbing *alpinisme* (m.)
close *près*
  very close *tout près*
  close to here *près d'ici*
close (to) *fermer*
  close a file (to) *fermer un fichier*
closet *placard* (m.)
clothing/clothes *vêtements* (m. pl.)
  clothing store *magasin* (m.) *de vêtements*
cloud *nuage* (m.)
cloudy *nuageux / nuageuse* (m./f.)
  It's cloudy. *C'est nuageux.*
club *boîte* (f.)
  nightclub *boîte de nuit*
  go out to clubs (to), go out clubbing
    (to) *sortir en boîte*
club (organization) *club* (m.)
coach *entraîneur* (m.)
coast *côte* (f.)
coat *manteau* (m.)
coffee *café* (m.)
  coffee with cream *café-crème* (m.)
  coffee shop *café* (m.)
coffeemaker *cafetière* (f.)
coincidence *coïncidence* (f.)
  What a coincidence! *Quelle coïncidence !*
cold *froid / froide* (m./f.)
  It's cold. *Il fait froid.*
  be cold (to) *avoir froid*
colleague *collègue / collègue* (m./f.)
collection *collection* (f.)
college *université* (f.)
  college degree *diplôme* (m.) *universitaire*
cologne *eau* (f.) *de Cologne*
come (to) *venir*
  come back (to) *revenir*
  come back (in) (to) *rentrer*

come in (to) *entrer*
come up (to) *monter*
come down (to) *descendre*
comedy *comédie* (f.)
   romantic comedy *comédie romantique*
comfortable *confortable*
company *société* (f.), *firme* (f.)
complicated *compliqué / compliquée* (m./f.)
computer *ordinateur* (m.)
concert *concert* (m.)
Congratulations. *Félicitations.*
consommé (clear soup made from
   stock) *consommé* (m.)
   vermicelli pasta consommé (noodle
      soup) *consommé aux vermicelles*
construction worker *ouvrier* (m.) *en bâtiment*
consult (to) *consulter*
cook *cuisinier / cuisinière* (m./f.)
cook (to) *cuisiner, préparer*
cooking *cuisine* (f.)
cool (good) *sympa*
corner *coin* (m.)
correct *exact / exacte* (m./f.)
cotton *coton* (m.)
couch *canapé* (m.)
counter *bar* (m.), *comptoir* (m.)
course *cours* (m.)
cousin *cousin / cousine* (m./f.)
cream, creamy dessert *crème* (f.)
   creamy dessert made with caramel *crème
      caramel*
crêpe (tissue-thin pancake) *crêpe* (f.)
   Crêpe Suzette *(crêpe with sugar, orange, and
      liqueur) crêpe Suzette*
crime drama/film *film* (m.) *policier*
cross (to) *traverser*
crudités (French appetizer of raw, mixed
   vegetables) *crudités* (f. pl.)
cucumber *concombre* (m.)
cup *tasse* (f.)
cupboard *placard* (m.)
curtain *rideau* (m.)

D

Dad/Daddy *papa*
daily *quotidien / quotidienne* (m./f.)
dance/dancing *danse* (f.)

dance (to) *danser*
daughter *fille* (f.)
daughter-in-law *belle-fille* (f.)
day *jour* (m.), *journée* (f.)
dear *cher / chère* (m./f.)
December *décembre*
decide (to) *décider*
degree *degré* (m.)
degree (college) *diplôme* (m.) *universitaire*
delete (to) *supprimer*
delicious *délicieux / délicieuse* (m./f.)
dentist *dentiste* (m.)
deodorant *déodorant* (m.)
department store *grand magasin* (m.)
descend (to) *descendre*
description *description* (f.)
desert *désert* (m.)
desk *bureau* (m.)
dessert *dessert* (m.)
detective (adjective) *policier / policière* (m./f.)
   detective drama/film *film* (m.) *policier*
detest (to) *détester*
device *appareil* (m.)
different *différent / différente* (m./f.)
difficult *difficile*
dine (to) *dîner*
dining room *salle* (f.) *à manger*
dinner *dîner* (m.)
   have dinner (to) *dîner*
diploma *diplôme* (m.)
direction *direction* (f.)
director *directeur / directrice* (m./f.)
dirty *sale*
dish *plat* (m.)
dishwasher *lave-vaisselle* (m.)
dishwashing detergent *liquide* (m.) *vaisselle*
do (to) *faire*
   do a tour (to) *faire un tour*
   do the cooking (to) *faire la cuisine*
   do the dishes (to) *faire la vaisselle*
   do the house cleaning (to) *faire le ménage*
   do the laundry (to) *faire la lessive*
   do the shopping (to) *faire les courses*
doctor *médecin* (m.), *docteur* (m.)
document *document* (m.)
documentary *documentaire* (m.)
dog *chien* (m.)
door *porte* (f.)

drama *drame* (m.)
drawer *tiroir* (m.)
dress *robe* (f.)
dress oneself (to) *s'habiller*
drink *boisson* (f.)
drink (to) *boire*
drive (computer) *lecteur* (m.)
  CD-ROM drive *lecteur de CD-ROM*
drugstore *pharmacie* (f.)
dryer *sèche-linge* (m.)
dubbed *doublé / doublée* (m./f.)
duck *canard* (m.)
  duck à l'orange, duck with orange
    sauce *canard à l'orange*
DVD player *lecteur* (m.) *de DVD*

E

each *chaque, chacun / chacune* (m./f.)
each one *chacun / chacune* (m./f.)
ear *oreille* (f.)
earn (to) *gagner*
earring *boucle* (f.) *d'oreille*
east *est* (m.)
easy *facile*
eat (to) *manger*
egg *œuf* (m.)
Eiffel Tower *Tour* (f.) *Eiffel*
eight *huit*
eighteen *dix-huit*
eighth *huitième*
eighty *quatre-vingts*
elbow *coude* (m.)
electrician *électricien* (m.)
electronic game *jeu* (m.) *électronique*
electronics store *magasin* (m.) *d'électronique*
eleven *onze*
email *mail* (m.), *mél* (m.), *email* (m.), *courriel* (m.),
  courrier (m.) *électronique*
employee *employé / employée* (m./f.)
employment *emploi* (m.)
end (to) *terminer*
engineer *ingénieur* (m.)
enjoyable *agréable*
enough *assez*
enter (to) *entrer*
entrance *entrée* (f.)
errand *course* (f.)

especially *surtout*
essential *essentiel / essentielle* (m./f.)
even *même*
evening *soir* (m.), *soirée* (f.)
  this evening *ce soir*
every *tout / toute* (m./f.), *chaque*
everyday *quotidien / quotidienne* (m./f.)
exact *exact / exacte* (m./f.)
excellent *excellent / excellente* (m./f.)
exciting *passionnant / passionnante* (m./f.)
excuse (to) *excuser*
  Excuse me. *Pardon.*
expensive *cher / chère* (m./f.)
expression *expression* (f.)
exterior *extérieur* (m.)
eye (eyes) *œil* (m.) *(yeux, pl.)*
eyebrow *sourcil* (m.)
eyeglasses *lunettes* (f. pl.)
eyelash *cil* (m.)

F

face *visage* (m.)
factory *usine* (f.)
fail (a test) (to) *rater (un examen)*
fall (season) *automne* (m.)
  in (the) fall *en automne*
fall (to) *tomber*
false *faux / fausse* (m./f.)
familiar with (to be) *connaître*
family *famille* (f.)
famous *célèbre*
Fantastic. *Formidable.*
far *loin*
  far from here *loin d'ici*
  farther *plus loin*
farmer *fermier / fermière* (m./f.)
fat *gros / grosse* (m./f.)
father *père* (m.)
  father-in-law *beau-père* (m.)
favorite *préféré / préférée* (m./f.)
fax machine *télécopieur* (m.)
February *février*
festival *fête* (f.)
fiancé/fiancée *fiancé / fiancée* (m./f.)
field *champ* (m.)
fifteen *quinze*
fifth *cinquième*

fifty *cinquante*
file *fichier* (m.)
film *film* (m.)
   action film *film d'action*
   crime/detective film, crime/detective
      drama *film policier*
   original version of a film (not dubbed into
      French) *version* (f.) *originale (v.o.)*
   French version of a film (dubbed into
      French) *version* (f.) *française (v.f.)*
final *dernier / dernière* (m./f.)
finally *enfin*
find (to) *trouver*
find oneself (somewhere) (to) *se trouver*
fine *bien*
finger *doigt* (m.)
finish (to) *finir, terminer*
fire *feu* (m.)
firm (company) *firme* (f.)
first *premier / première* (m./f.)
fish *poisson* (m.)
five *cinq*
flag *drapeau* (m.)
flavor *parfum* (m.)
floor *sol* (m.)
flower *fleur* (f.)
fog *brouillard* (m.)
food *nourriture* (f.)
foot *pied* (m.)
(American) football *football* (m.) *américain*
for *pour, de / d'*
forehead *front* (m.)
forest *forêt* (f.)
fork *fourchette* (f.)
forty *quarante*
forward (to) *faire suivre*
four *quatre*
fourteen *quatorze*
fourth *quatrième*
French *français / française* (m./f.)
   French language *français* (m.)
   French version of a film (dubbed into
      French) *version* (f.) *française (v.f.)*
   French fries *frites* (f. pl.)
Friday *vendredi*
friend *ami / amie* (m./f.)
friendly *amical / amicale* (m./f.)
from *de / d'*

   from here *d'ici*
fruit *fruit* (m.)
   fruit salad *salade* (f.) *de fruits*
full-time *à plein temps*
funny *amusant / amusante* (m./f.)

G

gallery *galerie* (f.)
game *jeu* (m.), *match* (m.)
garage *garage* (m.)
garden *jardin* (m.)
generous *généreux / généreuse* (m./f.)
gentle *doux / douce* (m./f.)
get a divorce (to) *divorcer*
get dressed (to) *s'habiller*
get somewhere (to) *arriver*
get up (to) *se lever*
girl *fille* (f.)
girlfriend *copine* (f.), *petite amie* (f.)
give (to) *donner*
glass *verre* (m.)
glove *gant* (m.)
go (to) *aller*
   Let's go. *Allons-y. / On y va.*
   go across (to) *traverser*
   go away (to) *partir*
   go down (to) *descendre*
   go horseback riding (to) *faire de l'équitation*
   go swimming (to) *faire de la natation*
   go camping (to) *camper*
   go hiking (to) *faire de la marche, de la randonée*
   go home (to) *rentrer*
   go in (to) *rentrer*
   go out (to) *partir*
   go out clubbing (to), go out to clubs
      (to) *sortir en boîte*
   go (past) (to) *passer*
   go shopping (to) *faire les courses*
   go sightseeing (to) *aller visiter*
   go to bed (to) *se coucher*
   go up (to) *monter*
good *bon / bonne* (m./f.), *bien, sympa*
   very good *très bien, très bon / bonne,*
      très sympa
   Good luck. *Bonne chance.*
   Good evening. *Bonsoir.*
   Good-bye. *Au revoir.*

grade *note (score)* (f.)
grammar *grammaire* (f.)
grandfather *grand-père* (m.)
  grandfather clock *pendule* (f.)
grandmother *grand-mère* (f.)
grandparent *grand-parent* (m.)
grape(s) *raisin* (m.)
Great. *Super.*
green *vert / verte* (m./f.)
  green bean *haricot* (m.) *vert*
guide *guide* (m.)
guided tour *visite* (f.) *guidée*
gym (physical education) *gymnastique* (f.)
gymnastics *gymnastique* (f.)

H

hail *grêle* (f.)
  It's hailing. *Il grêle.*
hair *cheveux* (m. pl.)
  hair (single strand) *cheveu* (m.)
half *demi / demie* (m./f.)
  half past ... *... et demie*
hall *couloir* (m.), *salle* (f.)
hand *main* (f.)
handsome *beau / bel / belle* (m./m. before vowel or silent h/f.)
happy *heureux / heureuse* (m./f.)
haste *hâte* (f.)
hasten (to) *hâter*
hat *chapeau* (m.)
hate (to) *détester*
hatred *haine* (f.)
have (to) *avoir*
  have (food/drink) (to) *prendre*
  have a drink (to) *prendre un verre*
  have breakfast (to) *prendre le petit déjeuner*
  have lunch (to) *déjeuner*
  have dinner (to) *dîner*
  have a good time (to), have fun (to) *s'amuser*
  have a party (to) *organiser une fête*
he *il*
head *tête* (f.)
health *santé* (f.)
  To your health! *À votre santé !*
  healthy *en bonne santé*
heart *cœur* (m.)

Hello. *Bonjour.*
  Hello. (on the phone) *Allô.*
her *son / sa / ses* (m./f./pl.), *elle*
here *ici, ci*
  from here *d'ici*
  here is/are, here it is/they are *voici, voilà*
hero/heroine *héros / héroïne* (m./f.)
herself (reflexive pronoun) *se / s'*
Hi. *Salut.*
high *haut / haute* (m./f.)
hill *colline* (f.)
him *lui*
himself (reflexive pronoun) *se / s'*
his *son / sa / ses* (m./f./pl.)
history *histoire* (f.)
hockey *hockey* (m.)
holiday *fête* (f.)
home *maison* (f.), *foyer* (m.)
homemade *maison*
homework *devoirs* (m. pl.)
honey *miel* (m.)
horseback riding *équitation* (f.)
  go horseback riding (to) *faire de l'équitation*
hospital *hôpital* (m.)
hot *chaud / chaude* (m./f.)
  It's hot./It's warm. *Il fait chaud.*
  be hot/warm (to) *avoir chaud*
hotel *hôtel* (m.)
hour *heure* (f.)
house cleaning *ménage* (m.)
house *maison* (f.)
  at someone's house/place *chez*
how *comment, comme*
  how many, how much *combien*
  How? (Pardon?/What did you say?) *Comment ?*
  How's it going?/How are you? *(Comment) ça va ?*
  How are you? *Comment vas-tu ?* (infml.) / *Comment allez-vous ?* (pl./fml.)
hundred *cent*
hunger *faim* (f.)
  be hungry (to) *avoir faim*
hurricane *ouragan* (m.)
husband *mari* (m.)

I

I *je / j'*
I am called ... (My name is ...) *Je m'appelle...*
I don't understand. *Je ne comprends pas.*
I'm fine. *Ça va.*
I'm very well. *Je vais très bien.*
I want ... *Je veux...*
I would like ... *Je voudrais...*
ice skate/skating *patin* (m.) *à glace*
idea *idée* (f.)
if *si*
Île de la Cité (City Island) *Île* (f.) *de la Cité*
impoverished *pauvre*
in *à, dans, en*
   in the *au / à la / à l' / aux* (m./f./m. or f. before a
      vowel or silent h/pl.)
   in front (of) *devant*
indeed *en effet*
information center *centre* (m.) *d'informations*
inherit (to) *hériter*
inn *auberge* (f.)
instant message *message* (m.) *instantané*
intelligent *intelligent / intelligente* (m./f.)
interesting *intéressant / intéressante* (m./f.)
internet *Internet* (m.)
intersection *intersection* (f.)
into *dans, en*
introduce (to) *présenter*
   Let me introduce ... *Je te présente...* (infml.) /
      Je vous présente... (pl./fml.)
invite (to) *inviter*
iron *fer* (m.) *à repasser*
ironing board *planche* (f.) *à repasser*
Is that all? *C'est tout ?*
isn't it?/isn't that so? *n'est-ce pas ?*
it *ça / c', il / elle / ils / elles* (m./f./m. pl./f. pl.)
   It rains. *Il pleut.*
it is *c'est*
   isn't it? *n'est-ce pas ?*
   it's necessary to *il faut*
   It's going well. *Ça va bien.*
   It's not going well./It's going badly. *Ça va
      mal.*
   It's beautiful (outside). *Il fait beau.*
   It's hot./It's warm. *Il fait chaud.*
   It's cold. *Il fait froid.*
   It's sunny. *Il fait (du) soleil.*

   It's windy. *Il fait du vent. / Il y a du vent.*
   It's hailing. *Il grêle.*
   It's snowing. *Il neige.*
   It's raining. *Il pleut.*
its *son / sa / ses* (m./f./pl.)
itself (reflexive pronoun) *se / s'*

J

jacket *veste* (f.)
January *janvier*
jeans *jean* (m.)
jewel *bijou* (m.)
   jewelry *bijoux* (m. pl.)
job *boulot* (m.), *emploi* (m.)
joint (of meat) *rôti* (m.)
journalist *journaliste* (m./f.)
juice *jus* (m.)
July *juillet*
June *juin*
junior high school *collège* (m.)

K

keyboard *clavier* (m.)
kind *gentil / gentille* (m./f.)
kitchen *cuisine* (f.)
   kitchen sink *évier* (m.) *de la cuisine*
knee *genou* (m.)
knife *couteau* (m.)
know (to) *savoir, connaître*

L

lake *lac* (m.)
lamb *agneau* (m.)
lamp *lampe* (f.)
lamppost *réverbère* (m.)
land *terre* (f.)
language *langue* (f.)
large *grand / grande* (m./f.)
last *dernier / dernière* (m./f.)
latest *dernier / dernière* (m./f.)
laundry detergent *lessive* (f.)
lawyer *avocat / avocate* (m./f.)
learn (to) *apprendre*
   I'm learning French. *J'apprends le français.*
leather *cuir* (m.)

leave (to) *partir, sortir*
left *gauche* (f.)
leg *jambe* (f.)
less *moins*
lesson *leçon* (f.)
Let me introduce ... *Je te présente...* (infml.) / *Je vous présente...* (pl./fml.)
Let's go. *Allons-y.* / *On y va.* (infml.)
letter *lettre* (f.)
lettuce *laitue* (f.)
library *bibliothèque* (f.)
life *vie* (f.)
lightning *éclair* (m.)
like *comme*
like (to) *aimer*
line *queue* (f.)
   wait in line (to) *faire la queue*
link *liaison* (f.)
listen (to) (to) *écouter*
literature *littérature* (f.)
little *petit / petite* (m./f.)
   a little *un peu*
live (to) *habiter*
living room *salon* (m.)
lobster *homard* (m.)
   lobster bisque *bisque* (f.) *de homard*
long *long / longue* (m./f.)
look for (to) *chercher*
look forward to (to) (can't wait) *avoir hâte*
lose (to) *perdre*
lost *perdu / perdue* (m./f.)
   I'm lost. *Je suis perdu / perdue.*
Louvre *Louvre* (m.)
love (to) *aimer, adorer*
low *bas / basse* (m./f.)
lunch *déjeuner* (m.)
   have lunch (to) *déjeuner*
lung *poumon* (m.)

M

ma'am/madam *madame*
magazine *magazine* (m.), *revue* (f.)
mail *poste* (f.)
mail (to) *mettre à la poste*
main course/dish *plat* (m.) *principal*
make (to) *faire, préparer*
   make a phone call (to) *téléphoner*

   That makes ... *Ça fait...*
man *homme* (m.)
manager *gérant / gérante* (m./f.), *directeur / directrice* (m./f.)
many *beaucoup de*
map *carte* (f.), *plan* (m.)
March *mars*
market *marché* (m.)
marry (someone) (to) *épouser (quelqu'un)*
match (in sports) *match* (m.)
math *maths* (f.), *mathématiques* (f.)
May *mai*
mayor *maire* (m.)
me *moi*
meat *viande* (f.)
medicine *médecine* (f.)
   medicine cabinet *armoire* (f.) *à pharmacie*
meet (a person/someone) (to) *rencontrer (une personne/quelqu'un)*
meeting *rendez-vous* (m.), *réunion* (f.)
   meeting room *salle* (f.) *de réunion*
melon *melon* (m.)
memory *mémoire* (f.)
menu *menu* (m.), *carte* (f.)
metro *métro* (m.)
   metro station *station* (f.) *de métro*
microwave (oven) *micro-ondes* (m.)
middle school *collège* (m.)
midnight *minuit* (m.)
milk *lait* (m.)
minus *moins*
mirror *miroir* (m.)
miss *mademoiselle*
modem *modem* (m.)
Mom/Mommy *maman*
moment *moment* (m.)
Mona Lisa *Joconde* (f.)
Monday *lundi*
monitor *écran* (m.)
month *mois* (m.)
monument *monument* (m.)
moon *lune* (f.)
more *plus*
morning *matin* (m.), *matinée* (f.)
mosque *mosquée* (f.)
mostly *surtout*
mother *mère* (f.)
   mother-in-law *belle-mère* (f.)

motorcycle/motorcycling *moto* (f.)
mountain *montagne* (f.)
mouse *souris* (f.)
mousse *mousse* (f.)
mouth *bouche* (f.)
movie *film* (m.)
  movie theater, the movies *cinéma* (m.)
Mr. *monsieur*
Mrs. *madame*
Ms. *madame*
municipal building *mairie* (f.)
muscle *muscle* (m.)
museum *musée* (m.)
music *musique* (f.)
musician *musicien / musicienne* (m./f.)
my *mon / ma / mes* (m./f./pl.)
  My name is … *Je m'appelle…*
myself (reflexive pronoun) *me / m'*
mysterious *mystérieux / mystérieuse* (m./f.)

N

name *nom* (m.)
napkin *serviette* (f.)
near *près*
  very near *tout près*
  nearby, near here *près d'ici*
necessary (to be) *falloir*
neck *cou* (m.)
necklace *collier* (m.)
neighborhood *quartier* (m.), *coin* (m.)
nephew *neveu* (m.)
never *jamais*
new *nouveau / nouvel / nouvelle* (m./m. before a vowel or silent h/f.)
news (the news) *nouvelles* (f. pl.)
next *ensuite*
  next to *à côté de*
nice *gentil / gentille* (m./f.), *sympa, joli / jolie* (m./f.), *beau / bel / belle* (m./m. before vowel or silent h/f.)
  Nice to meet you. *Enchanté. / Enchantée.* (m./f.)
niece *nièce* (f.)
night *nuit* (f.), *soir* (m.)
nightclub *boîte de nuit* (f.)
  go out to clubs (to), go out clubbing (to) *sortir en boîte*

nine *neuf*
nineteen *dix-neuf*
ninety *quatre-vingt-dix*
ninth *neuvième*
no *non*
noodle soup (vermicelli pasta consommé) *consommé* (m.) *aux vermicelles*
noon *midi* (m.)
north *nord* (m.)
nose *nez* (m.)
not *ne / n'… pas, pas*
  Not bad. *Pas mal.*
note *note* (f.)
notebook *cahier* (m.)
nothing *rien*
  It's nothing. *De rien.*
November *novembre*
now *maintenant*
number *nombre* (m.)

O

ocean *océan* (m.)
October *octobre*
of *de / d'*
  of it, of them *en*
  of the *du / de la / de l' / des* (m./f./m. or f. before a vowel or silent h/pl.)
  Of course. *Bien sûr.*
office *bureau* (m.)
oil *huile* (f.)
Okay. *D'accord.*
old *vieux / vieil / vieille* (m./m. before a vowel or silent h/f.)
once *une fois*
one (number) *un / une* (m./f.)
one (pronoun) *on*
oneself (reflexive pronoun) *se / s'*
onion *oignon* (m.)
  onion soup *soupe* (f.) *à l'oignon*
only child *fils / fille unique* (m./f.)
open (to) *ouvrir*
  open a file (to) *ouvrir un fichier*
opera *opéra* (m.)
or *ou*
orange *orange* (f.)
organize (to) *organiser*
original *original / originale* (m./f.)

original version of a film (not dubbed into French) *version* (f.) *originale (v.o.)*
other *autre*
our *notre / nos* (m. or f./pl.)
ourselves (reflexive pronoun) *nous*
outside (preposition) *hors*
outside (noun) *extérieur* (m.)
oven *four* (m.)
over there *là-bas*
own *propre*

P

paint (to) *peindre*
painting *tableau* (m.)
pajamas *pyjama* (m.)
pants *pantalon* (m.)
Pardon (me). *Pardon.*
parent *parent* (m.)
Paris *Paris*
park *parc* (m.)
part (in a play, movie, etc.) *rôle* (m.)
part-time *à temps partiel*
party *soirée* (f.), *fête* (f.), *partie* (f.)
pass (to) *passer*
    pass (a test) (to) *réussir à (un examen)*
passport *passeport* (m.)
pastry *pâtisserie* (f.)
    pastry shop *pâtisserie* (f.)
pâté (spreadable purée of meat) *pâté* (m.)
pay (to) *payer*
peach *pêche* (f.)
    peaches with ice cream *pêche Melba*
pear *poire* (f.)
people *gens* (m. pl.)
people in general (pronoun) *on*
pepper (condiment) *poivre* (m.)
pepper (vegetable) *poivron* (m.)
perfect *parfait / parfaite* (m./f.)
perform (to) *jouer*
perfume *parfum* (m.)
person *personne* (f.)
pharmacy *pharmacie* (f.)
phone (to) *téléphoner*
photo *photo* (f.)
    Can you take our picture (photo), please? *Pourriez-vous nous prendre en photo, s'il vous plaît ?*

physical education *gymnastique* (f.)
piece *pièce* (f.)
pig *porc* (m.), *cochon* (m.)
place *place* (f.)
plant *plante* (f.)
plastic *plastique* (m.)
    made of plastic *en plastique*
plate *assiette* (f.)
play (theater) *pièce* (f.)
play (to) *jouer*
    play a sport (to) *faire du sport*
player (CDs, DVDs, etc.) *lecteur* (m.)
    CD player *lecteur de CD*
    DVD player *lecteur de DVD*
player (games, sports, etc.) *joueur / joueuse* (m./f.)
playing cards *cartes* (f. pl.) *à jouer*
pleasant *agréable*
please (infml./pl., fml.) *s'il te plaît / s'il vous plaît*
Pleased to meet you. *Enchanté. / Enchantée.* (m./f.)
pleasure *plaisir* (m.)
    With pleasure. *Avec plaisir.*
plumber *plombier* (m.)
police (adjective) *policier / policière* (m./f.)
policeman/woman *policier / femme policier* (m./f.)
pond *étang* (m.), *mare* (f.)
pool (billiards) *billard* (m.)
poor *pauvre*
pork *porc* (m.)
    pork chop *côte* (f.) *de porc*
post office *poste* (f.), *bureau* (m.) *de poste*
potato *pomme* (f.) *de terre*
powder *poudre* (f.), *talc* (m.)
practice (to) *pratiquer*
prefer (to) *préférer*
prepare (to) *préparer*
present (to) *présenter*
pretty *joli / jolie* (m./f.)
printer *imprimante* (f.)
professor *professeur / professeure* (m./f.)
professor (infml.) *prof* (m./f.)
progress *progrès* (m.)
purple *violet / violette* (m./f.)
put (to) *mettre*
    put in the mail (to) *mettre à la poste*

Q

quarter *quart* (m.)
  quarter after/past ... *... et quart*
  quarter to ... *... moins le quart*
quiche *quiche* (f.)
  type of quiche made with bacon *quiche lorraine*
quiet *calme*
quite *assez*

R

race *course* (f.)
rack (of meat) *carré* (m.)
  rack of lamb *carré d'agneau*
radish *radis* (m.)
rain *pluie* (f.)
rain (to) *pleuvoir*
  It's raining./It rains. *Il pleut.*
raw *cru / crue* (m./f.)
razor *rasoir* (m.)
reach (to) *arriver*
read (to) *lire*
ready *prêt / prête* (m./f.)
real *vrai / vraie* (m./f.)
really *en effet, bien*
recent *dernier / dernière* (m./f.)
reception desk *réception* (f.)
recess *récré(ation)* (f.)
red *rouge*
  red wine *vin* (m.) *rouge*
refrigerator *réfrigérateur* (m.)
relative *parent* (m.)
repeat (to) *répéter*
  Repeat (that), please. *Répétez, s'il vous plaît.*
reply (to) *répondre*
report card *bulletin* (m.) *scolaire*
reservation *réservation* (f.)
reserve (to) *réserver*
restaurant *restaurant* (m.)
restroom *toilettes* (f. pl.)
  Where is the restroom? *Où sont les toilettes ?*
retired *à la retraite*
retirement *retraite* (f.)
return (to) *revenir, rentrer*
reunion *réunion* (f.)
rib (meat) *côte* (f.)

rice *riz* (m.)
rich *riche*
right (opposite of left) *droite* (f.)
  be right (to) *avoir raison*
  right? *n'est-ce pas ?*
ring *bague* (f.)
rise (to) *monter*
river *rivière* (f.)
roast (of meat) *rôti* (m.)
roast(ed) *rôti / rôtie* (m./f.)
rock *rocher* (m.)
role *rôle* (m.)
romantic *romantique*
  romantic comedy *comédie* (f.) *romantique*
room *pièce* (f.), *salle* (f.), *place* (f.)
rosé wine *vin* (m.) *rosé*
run *course* (f.)
running *course à pied*
rural *rural / rurale* (m./f.)
rush (to) *se hâter*

S

Sacré Cœur (Sacred Heart) *Sacré-Cœur* (m.)
sad *triste*
sailing *voile* (f.)
salad *salade* (f.)
salary *salaire* (m.)
salesman/woman *vendeur / vendeuse* (m./f.)
salt *sel* (m.)
same *même*
sand *sable* (m.)
sardines *sardines* (f. pl.)
  sardines in tomato sauce *sardines sauce tomate*
Saturday *samedi*
sauce *sauce* (f.)
save a document (to) *sauvegarder un document*
scarf (fashion) *foulard* (m.)
scarf (winter) *écharpe* (f.)
scary *effrayant / effrayante* (m./f.)
schedule *horaire* (m.)
school *école* (f.)
screen *écran* (m.)
sculpture *sculpture* (f.)
sea *mer* (f.)
seat *place* (f.)
seated *assis / assise* (m./f.)

second *deuxième, second / seconde* (m./f.)
secondary school *collège* (m.)
secretary *secrétaire* (m./f.)
see (to) *voir*
sell (to) *vendre*
send (to) *envoyer*
  send a file (to) *envoyer un fichier*
  send an email (to) *envoyer un mail / mél /
  email / courriel / courrier électronique*
September *septembre*
server *serveur / serveuse* (m./f.)
seven *sept*
seventeen *dix-sept*
seventh *septième*
seventy *soixante-dix*
shame *honte* (f.)
  be ashamed (to) *avoir honte*
shampoo *shampooing* (m.)
shave (to) *se raser*
shaving cream *crème* (f.) *à raser*
she *elle*
shelf *étagère* (f.)
shirt *chemise* (f.)
shoe *chaussure* (f.)
  shoe store *magasin* (m.) *de chaussures*
short *petit / petite* (m./f.), *court / courte* (m./f.)
shoulder *épaule* (f.)
show (to) *montrer, présenter, donner*
shower *douche* (f.)
shower gel *gel* (m.) *douche*
shrimp *crevettes* (f. pl.)
sick *malade*
side *côté* (m.)
  next to (at the side of) *à côté de*
sidewalk *trottoir* (m.)
silk *soie* (f.)
sing (to) *chanter*
singer *chanteur / chanteuse* (m./f.)
sink *évier* (m.)
sir *monsieur*
sister *sœur* (f.)
sitting (down) *assis / assise* (m./f.)
situated (to be) *se trouver*
six *six*
sixteen *seize*
sixth *sixième*
sixty *soixante*
size *taille* (f.)

skate/skating *patin* (m.)
skiing *ski* (m.)
skin *peau* (f.)
skirt *jupe* (f.)
sky *ciel* (m.)
sleeping car/sleeper car *wagon-lit* (m.)
sleepy (to be) *avoir sommeil*
slow *lent / lente* (m./f.)
slowly *lentement*
small *petit / petite* (m./f.)
smile *sourire* (m.)
sneaker *basket* (m./f.), *chaussure* (f.) *de basket*
snow *neige* (f.)
snow (to) *neiger*
  It's snowing. *Il neige.*
so ... *alors...*
soap *savon* (m.)
soccer *foot(ball)* (m.)
  soccer player *footballeur / footballeuse* (m./f.)
  soccer stadium *stade* (m.) *de foot*
social *social / sociale* (m./f.)
sock *chaussette* (f.)
sofa *canapé* (m.)
soft *doux / douce* (m./f.)
soft drink *boisson* (f.) *gazeuse*
sole (fish) *sole* (f.)
  sole covered in flour and sautéed in
    butter *sole meunière*
some *du / de la / de l' / des* (m./f./m. or f. before a
  vowel or silent h/pl.), *en*
sometimes *parfois*
son *fils* (m.)
son-in-law *beau-fils* (m.)
song *chanson* (f.)
So-so. *Comme ci, comme ça.*
sound system *chaîne* (f.) *hi-fi*
soup *soupe* (f.)
  onion soup *soupe à l'oignon*
  consommé (clear soup made from
    stock) *consommé* (m.)
  vermicelli pasta consommé (noodle
    soup) *consommé aux vermicelles*
sour *aigre*
south *sud* (m.)
speak (to) *parler*
  Speak more slowly, please. *Parlez plus lente-
    ment, s'il vous plaît.*

I speak a little French. *Je parle un peu français.*

specialty *spécialité* (f.)

spoon *cuillère* (f.)

spring *printemps* (m.)

   in (the) spring *au printemps*

square *carré* (m.)

stadium *stade* (m.)

   soccer stadium *stade de foot*

staff *personnel* (m.)

stairs *escaliers* (m. pl.)

stamp *timbre* (m.)

standing (up) *debout*

star *étoile* (f.)

start (to) *commencer*

station *station* (f.)

   subway/metro station *station de métro*

statue *statue* (f.)

stay (to) *rester*

steady job *emploi* (m.) *régulier*

stepdaughter *belle-fille* (f.)

stepfather *beau-père* (m.)

stepmother *belle-mère* (f.)

stepson *beau-fils* (m.)

still *toujours*

stomach *estomac* (m.)

stop *arrêt* (m.)

   bus stop *arrêt de bus*

store *magasin* (m.)

storm *orage* (m.)

story *histoire* (f.)

stove *cuisinière* (f.)

straight *droit*

   straight ahead *tout droit*

street *rue* (f.)

streetlight *lampadaire* (m.)

strong *fort / forte* (m./f.)

student *étudiant / étudiante* (m./f.)

study (to) *étudier*

subject *sujet* (m.)

subtitle *sous-titre* (m.)

suburban *de banlieue*

suburbs *banlieue* (f.)

subway *métro* (m.)

   subway station *station* (f.) *de métro*

sugar *sucre* (m.)

suit *costume* (m.)

summer *été* (m.)

   in (the) summer *en été*

sun *soleil* (m.)

   It's sunny. *Il fait (du) soleil.*

Sunday *dimanche*

sunglasses *lunettes* (f. pl.) *de soleil*

Super. *Super.*

supermarket *supermarché* (m.)

sweet *doux / douce* (m./f.)

swimming *natation* (f.)

   go swimming (to) *faire de la natation*

Swiss *suisse*

synagogue *synagogue* (f.)

T

table *table* (f.)

   table for two *table pour deux*

tail *queue* (f.)

take (to) *prendre*

   take a bath (to) *prendre un bain*

   take a shower (to) *prendre une douche*

   take a tour (to) *faire un tour*

   take along (to) *emmener*

   take a picture (to) *prendre une photo*

   Can you take our picture? *Pourriez-vous nous prendre en photo, s'il vous plaît ?*

talented *talentueux / talentueuse* (m./f.)

talk (to) *parler*

tall *grand / grande* (m./f.)

taste *goût* (m.)

taxi *taxi* (m.)

   taxi driver *chauffeur* (m.) *de taxi*

tea *thé* (m.)

teach (to) *enseigner*

teacher *professeur / professeure* (m./f.), *enseignant / enseignante* (m./f.)

teacher (infml.) *prof* (m./f.)

teakettle/teapot *théière* (f.)

team *équipe* (f.)

teenager *adolescent / adolescente* (m./f.)

telephone *téléphone* (m.), *appareil* (m.)

television *télé(vision)* (f.)

   television program *émission* (f.)

temperature *température* (f.)

temple *temple* (m.)

ten *dix*

tendon *tendon* (m.)

tennis *tennis* (m.)

tennis shoe *basket* (m./f.), *chaussure* (f.) *de basket*
tenth *dixième*
test *examen* (m.)
  fail (a test) (to) *rater (un examen)*
  pass (a test) (to) *réussir à (un examen)*
textbook *livre* (m.) *scolaire*
thank you *merci*
that *ce / cet / cette* (m./m. before a vowel or silent h/f.), *ça / c'*, *que, qui*
  That makes .../That is *Ça fait...*
  that is *c'est*
  Is that all? *C'est tout ?*
the *le / la / l' / les* (m./f./m. or f. before a vowel or silent h/pl.)
theater *théâtre* (m.)
their *leur / leurs* (m. or f./pl.)
them *eux / elles* (m./f.)
themselves (reflexive pronoun) *se / s'*
then *puis, ensuite, alors*
there *là, là-bas*
  over there *là-bas*
  there is/are *il y a, voilà*
  there it is/they are *voilà*
these *ces*
they *ils / elles* (m./f.)
thin *mince*
thing *chose* (f.)
think (to) *penser*
third *troisième*
thirst *soif* (f.)
  be thirsty (to) *avoir soif*
thirteen *treize*
thirty *trente*
this *ce / cet / cette* (m./m. before a vowel or silent h/f.), *ça / c', ci*
this is *c'est*
those *ces*
thousand *mille*
three *trois*
throw (to) *envoyer*
thunder *tonnerre* (m.)
Thursday *jeudi*
ticket *place* (f.)
tie (in a game/match) (to) *faire match nul*
time *fois* (f.), *temps* (m.)
  once (one time) *une fois*
  What time is it? *Quelle heure est-il ?*

to *à, pour, en, jusqu'à*
  to the *au / à la / à l' / aux* (m./f./m. or f. before a vowel or silent h/pl.)
  next to *à côté de*
  To your health! *À votre santé !*
today *aujourd'hui*
toe *doigt* (m.) *de pied, orteil* (m.)
together *ensemble*
toilet *toilettes* (f. pl.)
  toilet paper *papier* (m.) *hygiénique*
tomato *tomate* (f.)
tomorrow *demain*
tongue *langue* (f.)
tonight *ce soir*
too *aussi*
tooth *dent* (f.)
tour *tour* (m.)
tourist *touriste* (m./f.)
towel *serviette* (f.)
  bath towel *serviette de bain*
tower *tour* (f.)
  Eiffel Tower *Tour Eiffel*
town *ville* (f.)
traffic *circulation* (f.)
train *train* (m.)
  train station *gare* (f.)
travel (to) *voyager*
tree *arbre* (m.)
trout *truite* (f.)
  trout cooked in wine and vinegar *truite au bleu*
true *vrai / vraie* (m./f.)
T-shirt *T-shirt* (m.)
Tuesday *mardi*
turn *tour* (m.)
turn (to) *tourner*
TV *télé(vision)* (f.)
twelve *douze*
twenty *vingt*
two *deux*

U

ugly *laid / laide* (m./f.)
umbrella *parapluie* (m.)
uncle *oncle* (m.)
underpants *caleçon* (m.)
undershirt *maillot* (m.) *de corps*

understand (to) *comprendre*
  I don't understand. *Je ne comprends pas.*
underwear *sous-vêtements* (m. pl.)
unemployed *au chômage, sans emploi*
unemployment *chômage* (m.)
unfriendly *peu amical / peu amicale* (m./f.)
university *université* (f.)
until, up until, up to *jusqu'à*
urban *urbain / urbaine* (m./f.)
us *nous*

V

vacation *vacances* (f. pl.)
vain *vain / vaine* (m./f.)
vegetable *légume* (m.)
vermicelli pasta *vermicelle* (m.)
  vermicelli pasta consommé (noodle
    soup) *consommé* (m.) *aux vermicelles*
version *version* (f.)
very *très, bien*
  very good *très bien, très bon / bonne* (m./f.)
  very well *très bien*
veterinarian *vétérinaire* (m.)
video game *jeu* (m.) *vidéo*
Vietnamese *vietnamien / vietnamienne* (m./f.)
village *village* (m.)
violin *violon* (m.)
visit (a place) (to) *visiter*
vocabulary *vocabulaire* (m.)

W

wait in line (to) *faire la queue*
waiter/waitress *serveur / serveuse* (m./f.)
wall *mur* (m.)
want (to) *vouloir*
  I want ... *Je veux...*
wardrobe *armoire* (f.)
warm *chaud / chaude* (m./f.)
  It's warm./It's hot. *Il fait chaud.*
  be warm/hot (to) *avoir chaud*
wash (to) *laver*
  wash up (to), wash oneself (to) *se laver*
washing machine *machine* (f.) *à laver,
  lave-linge* (m.)
washroom *salle* (f.) *de bains*
watch *montre* (f.)

watch (to) *regarder*
water *eau* (f.)
way *direction* (f.)
  this way *par ici*
we *nous, on* (infml.)
weak *faible*
wear (to) *porter*
weather *temps* (m.)
  What is the weather today? *Quel temps fait-
    il aujourd'hui ?*
webpage *page* (f.) *web*
website *site* (m.) *web*
Wednesday *mercredi*
week *semaine* (f.)
weekend *week-end* (m.)
weight lifting *haltérophilie* (f.)
Welcome. *Bienvenue.*
  You're welcome. *De rien. / Je vous en prie.*
    (fml.)
well *bien*
  very well *très bien*
  It's going well. *Ça va bien.*
  Well done. *Bravo.*
well ... *alors...*
west *ouest* (m.)
what *qu'est-ce que, quel / quelle* (m./f.), *quoi, que*
  What is this/that? *Qu'est-ce que c'est ?*
  What is the weather today? *Quel temps fait-
    il aujourd'hui ?*
  What time is it? *Quelle heure est-il ?*
  What's your name? (pl./fml.) *Comment vous
    appelez-vous ?*
  What's your name? (infml.) *Comment
    t'appelles-tu ?*
where *où*
  Where is ... ? *Où se trouve... ? / Où est... ?*
  Where is the restroom? *Où sont les toilettes ?*
which *que, quel / quelle* (m./f.)
white *blanc / blanche* (m./f.)
  white wine *vin* (m.) *blanc*
who *qui*
  Who is it?/Who's calling? *Qui est à
    l'appareil ?*
whom *que*
wife *femme* (f.)
win (to) *gagner*
wind *vent* (m.)
  It's windy. *Il fait du vent. / Il y a du vent.*

window *fenêtre* (f.)
wine *vin* (m.)
  red/white/rosé wine *vin rouge / blanc / rosé*
  wine list *carte* (f.) *des vins*
winter *hiver* (m.)
  in (the) winter *en hiver*
with *avec*
  With pleasure. *Avec plaisir.*
without *sans*
woman *femme* (f.)
wood *bois* (m.)
wooden *en bois*
word *mot* (m.)
work *travail* (m.)
work (to) *travailler*
wrist *poignet* (m.)
write (to) *écrire*
writer *écrivain* (m.) *(sometimes: écrivaine,* f.)
wrong *faux / fausse* (m./f.), *mal*
  be wrong (to): *avoir tort*

Y

year *an* (m.), *année* (f.)
yellow *jaune*
yes *oui, si (answer to negative question)*
yesterday *hier*
you *tu* (infml.), *vous* (pl./fml.), *toi* (infml.)
  you have to/need to/must *il faut*
You're welcome. *De rien. / Je vous en prie.* (fml.)
young *jeune*
your (infml.) *ton / ta / tes* (m./f./pl.)
your (pl./fml.) *votre / vos* (m. or f./pl.)
yourself (reflexive pronoun) *te / t'* (infml.), *vous*
  (fml.)
yourselves (reflexive pronoun) *vous*
youth hostel *auberge* (f.) *de jeunesse*

Z

zero *zéro*